# BLACK CHURCH
# IN THE SIXTIES

Hart M. Nelsen &
Anne Kusener Nelsen

THE UNIVERSITY PRESS OF KENTUCKY

ISBN: 0-8131-1324-5

Library of Congress Catalog Card Number: 74-18937

Copyright © 1975 by The University Press of Kentucky

A statewide cooperative scholarly publishing agency
serving Berea College, Centre College of Kentucky,
Eastern Kentucky University, Georgetown College,
Kentucky Historical Society, Kentucky State University,
Morehead State University, Murray State University,
Northern Kentucky State College, Transylvania University,
University of Kentucky, University of Louisville, and
Western Kentucky University.

*Editorial and Sales Offices:* Lexington, Kentucky 40506

for Noah and Nova

# CONTENTS

# ACKNOWLEDGMENTS

The cooperation of numerous persons made this study possible. A large portion of the volume incorporates work done by the first author while he held a 15-months National Science Foundation Faculty Fellowship (No. 69126). That part of the study incorporated valuable suggestions from John D. McCarthy, Ernest Q. Campbell, Mayer N. Zald, Leo Rigsby, and Kelly Miller Smith—all of Vanderbilt University—and Hugh P. Whitt of the University of Nebraska at Lincoln.

Other individuals have also been of inestimable help in this study. Raytha L. Yokley and Thomas W. Madron of Western Kentucky University encouraged the study in numerous ways. Both kindly gave permission to use data jointly collected under PHS Research Grant 1 RO1 MH 16573 from the National Institute of Mental Health. We owe thanks to NIMH for support of this data collection and analysis. The conclusions drawn by us can in no way be attributed to policy of NIMH. Additional support for this study was provided by the Research Fund Committee of The Catholic University of America (from a National Science Foundation Institutional Grant); thanks are extended to the committee and to Drs. James P. O'Connor, John J. Murphy, and Eugene R. Kennedy.

The help of black interviewers in collecting the Bowling Green data deserves special thanks (the 97 percent completion rate is testimony to the quality of their work). The interviewers were L. D. Britt, Sarah Davidson, Lynda Dickson, Debbie Hart, Artanzie Hayne, Edith Johnson, Dorothy Offutt, Lynda Proctor, Mamie Starks, and Shelby White. Other thanks go to Linda Logan, a superb coder, and Paul Messick, who gave valuable research assistance.

Several organizations and individuals gave us permission to use their data for secondary analysis. The identification of the 30 data sets and sources follows:

The Black Church As a Politicizing Agency. The data were collected in 1970-1971, Bowling Green, Kentucky.

A Study of Religious Participation, Project 849, Detroit Area Study, Gerhard Lenski, Director of the 1958 Survey. The data were supplied by the Survey Research Center of the University of Michigan, with permission from Gerhard Lenski.

The Public Images of Mental Health Services Study, collected for and directed by Dr. Jack Elinson, Dr. Elena Padilla, and Dr. Marvin E. Perkins. The data were supplied by the Research Archives of the Columbia University School of Public Health and Administrative Medicine, with permission of the investigators. The interpretations presented in this volume are ours.

Negro Political Attitudes, Gary T. Marx, Principal Investigator. The data were furnished by the Inter-University Consortium for Political Research, the University of Michigan.

The Roper Public Opinion Research Center, together with the Gallup Poll organization, for the following data sets (all American Institute of Public Opinion national surveys): Numbers 539 (November 1954), 580 (March 1957), 625 (February 1960), 642 (March 1961), 655 (February 1962), 658 (May 1962), 660 (June 1962), 673 (May 1963), 676 (August 1963), 681 (December 1963), 695 (July 1964), 706 (February 1965), 708 (March 1965), 710 (April 1965), 711 (May 1965), 734 (September 1966), 738 (December 1966), 742 (March 1967), 749 (August 1967), 757 (January 1968), 758 (February 1968), 760 (April 1968), 764 (June 1968), 766 (August 1968), and 780 and 781 (May 1969).

With gratitude we remember the encouragement given us in this research and other studies by Professors Samuel Blizzard and V. Jacque Voegeli. Finally, let us note our indebtedness to earlier researchers of the black church, especially Benjamin E. Mays and Joseph W. Nicholson whose landmark study *The Negro's Church* was published in 1933.

# 1:

# Introduction

The study of the black church and black religiosity offers a unique opportunity to sociologists.* The increasing education, urbanization, and migration of the black population have had observable effects on worship styles, types of ministry, social class differentiation of churches, and the like. Somewhat similar changes could be observed for religious phenomena of white Protestants, but the findings would be less dramatic, because rising educational levels and urban migration occurred for them over a longer period of time. More important, these findings would be less revealing, for the white church is but one of many white institutions. On the other hand, the black church was one of the few black institutions left relatively free by whites in its development and modification and thus a study of the black church and black religiosity might well reveal basic black attitudes toward society. In 1932 Donald Young commented: "The Negro and the immigrant churches have become the only formal institutions definitely controlled by themselves. Their political activities are no more extensive than the native white man wants them to be. Their education is provided in schools whose finances and policies are matters of grave concern to the dominant classes. ... Few white men, however, show more than an idle curiosity about the Negro's 'superstitions' and 'primitive' religious observances."[1]

*By *religiosity* we mean *the state of being religious* rather than *excessive or affected piety,* although the latter is not excluded by our definition. Religiosity, then, consists of religious behaviors and attitudes on the part of individuals, and, here, specifically black Americans.

A study in black religion (which means, in large part, black Protestantism) should give insight into the relationship which black Americans have with their society, as indicated, for example, by otherworldly versus thisworldly orientations. Such a study might also determine the degree to which social cohesion exists among black Americans themselves, or the degree to which the black church acts as a communal organization.

In an article published in 1964, Peter Rossi observed the need for additional research on the roles of ethnic groups and religious institutions and on their origins and maintenance. Rossi discussed numerous directions which race relations research might take, including examination of the forms of organization taken by black protest movements.[2] In 1971 Metzger commented that Rossi's call for research in black movements, the role of ethnicity, and the political aspects of racial change had basically gone unheeded. Metzger suggested that the lack of studies of the civil rights and black power movements had been due to a sociological bias favoring the consensus model of racial change and tending to ignore a conflict position in which racism is seen as part of the institutional makeup of the society. The favored (or assimilationist) perspective contains the assumption that American blacks desire racial integration and that "the rate of their assimilation is directly proportional to their access to the socializing agencies of the dominant culture."[3] The pluralist view, however, would not foresee the waning and eventual disappearance of the black church, since black institutions would retain their identities. The strength of these institutions would constitute a variable in itself, depending upon numerous factors, including the degree to which blacks believe an integrated society is possible and how near this dream is.

### Black Religiosity As Sectarian

Blacks have traditionally been viewed as sectarian in their religious orientation. Argyle, for example, has commented, "Minority groups are often underprivileged and show an above-average level of religious activity, especially in sect religion, as in the instance of the American Negroes."[4] In a similar vein Marden and Meyer in 1962 commented that the black church in the South was fundamentalist in religious ideology and that its escapist appeal was due to frustrations over the caste status of its members.[5]

The fact that most black church members are Baptist encourages the sectarian interpretation by whites who interpret this denominational complex (the National Baptist Convention of the U.S.A., the National Baptist Convention of America, and the Progressive Baptist Convention) in the light of their understanding of the Southern Baptist orientations of whites.[6] For example, Hill has described the evangelical ministry, the emphasis on the experiential dimension of religiosity for individuals, and the neglect of social issues among southern whites and, especially, Southern Baptists.[7]

In viewing the black church within the sect-church framework, many sociologists readily write it off as not concerned with social problems.* Nelsen and Yokley have noted that the "church-sect typology posits a basically conservative orientation of the church toward social issues," since the church's role is adaptive and accommodative and since the sect's role is one of withdrawal, looking to immediate experience (as in conversion) and to the next world at the same time.[8] The perspective of this typology thus admits of little chance for the religious organization as an agency of social change. A different view is sometimes taken, however, notably in the study by Hammond and Mitchell of the Protestant campus ministry, which they hold represents a segment of radicalism,[9] and in the monograph by Fauset, who viewed the black religious organization of the metropolis as "likely to witness a transformation from its purely religious function to functions which will accommodate the urgent social needs of the Negro masses under modern stresses of politics and economics."[10]

---

*The church is the form of the religious organization which compromises itself in its basic acceptance and willingness to work within the secular society, while the sect rejects the secular order. Characteristics of the churchlike and sectlike religious orientations have been outlined by Liston Pope (*Millhands and Preachers* [New Haven: Yale University Press, 1942], pp. 122-24) and operationalized by Russell R. Dynes ("Church-Sect Typology and Socio-Economic Status," *American Sociological Review* 20 [October 1955]: 556-57). Built into this sect-church dichotomy is a bias for labeling the religious organization (whether church or sect) as inhibiting social change, since, by definition, the church tends to endorse the status quo of secular society, while the sect tends to reject involvement in the politics (and social issues) of the society.

Scholars acquainted with the church-sect typology too quickly project from this knowledge of the ideology of white sectarianism a unidimensionality for the religious beliefs of blacks, including such diverse attributes as preference for emotional worship, a literal interpretation of the scripture, and an unwillingness for the religious organization to "meddle" in political matters. The compatibility of a conservative religious outlook (for example, one having a traditional view of the Bible) with a concern for solving race problems would probably be dismissed by white and black sociologists alike.[11]

Furthermore, an interpretation of black religion as sectarian and otherworldly would seem logical at first glance since black religious practices and beliefs seemingly would still be influenced by the rural origins of the church members (many of whom are first- or second-generation city dwellers) and by the effects of the disorganization of city life, felt most acutely by migrants to the city according to the cultural shock theory introduced by Holt.[12] A rural background seemingly is coupled with a more conservative religious ideology; for example, it is reported that rural whites are more likely than urban whites to hold conservative, or fundamentalist, religious beliefs in today's society.[13] According to Holt's cultural shock thesis, storefront churches with an otherworldly orientation arose in the city as the result of the migration of rural people into urban areas. "This religious movement is largely the natural product of the social disorganization and cultural conflict which have attended the over-rapid urbanward migration and concomitant urbanization of an intensely rural, and among other things, religious fundamentalist population. . . . The movement is typically a social movement in that it is an attempt on the part of certain groups experiencing acute social maladjustment to recapture their sense of security through religious revival and reform."[14]

The theory has been criticized by several researchers who have supported their arguments with data collected mainly from whites. From an analysis of data collected in Columbus, Ohio, Dynes reported that the sectarians of his sample were characterized as having almost the longest period of residence, and he concluded that "the significance of sectarianism lies in its association with lower socioeconomic status."[15] From a secondary analysis of Lenski's Detroit Area Study and Southern Appalachian Studies data collected in

1958, Nelsen and Whitt concluded, "It cannot be said that the migrant experiences cultural shock and turns to sectlike religious expressions."[16]

Yet various authors comment about the emotionalism and other-worldly orientations of black storefront churches and ascribe these characteristics to accommodative behavior on the part of black migrants to the city. For example, Pinkney writes: "Because of the widespread social disorganization accompanying the urbanization of Negroes, many of them continued to feel the need for outlets from the frustrations they faced. Therefore they sought refuge in 'storefront' churches and in the many cults which developed."[17]

In sum, most writers view the black church as "a safety valve where thwarted desires and emotions may be freely vented."[18] Indeed, one of the foremost researchers in this area, the late E. Franklin Frazier, viewed the black church as a "barrier to the integration of Negroes into the main currents of American life."[19] This view, held into the 1960s, was described by Young in 1932:

> There are Negro leaders who regret the hold of the Christian church on the American colored population. There is evidence that their task of leadership is made difficult by the colored churches, if their task is to bring better times to their people on earth. . . . The emotional outlet provided by services and revivals and the certainty of salvation through the rebirth of conversion make a colored following hard to hold to a non-religious organization or program. . . . No matter which way the intellectual Negro leader turns, he is blocked by the church, for the church is not in sympathy with intellectual programs and has the strength of being of, not for, the people.[20]

Only rarely have commentators remarked upon the protest side of black religion. Here double meanings of the spirituals and the presence of black ministers among insurrection leaders are noted.[21]

### Community and Church

In an analysis of the effects of ethnicity in politics, Lane, after noting the centrality of the church in the black community, indicates that the early religious orientation of immigrant and black groups reduced political interest and activity because "religion offered an otherworldly solace for temporal ills," among other reasons. But at a later stage, religion can indirectly whet the political appetite through the increased social interaction of church members as well as through their perception of self-interest in political matters.[22]

Aware of their self-interests and able to have some degree of control over their environment, modern day black Americans evince greater political interest and activity. Assimilation into the mainstream of American society, however, could have the opposite effect. Lane cites several studies indicating that upwardly mobile individuals of ethnic background exhibit lower levels of political activity and concludes that "assimilation tends to depoliticize groups when it breaks up the homogeneity of ethnic associational life."[23]

Ethnic communities vary in the degree of their institutional completeness, that is, in the development of a formal structure and of a network of interpersonal relations (including religious, political, and educational organizations) along with control of their own news media—the extreme case meeting all the needs of the members of the ethnic community. From an analysis of interview data collected in Montreal, Breton noted that the degree of institutional completeness of an ethnic community affected its ability to attract the immigrant into its social boundaries. After raising the question "Do the institutions of an ethnic community affect the social relations only of those who use them, or do they generate a social life that extends beyond the realm of the participants?" he concludes that "the presence of churches in a community is related to more in-group relations even among those who do not attend the ethnic church."[24] And further: "If there is at least one church in the community, a large proportion of the immigrant's personal relations are contained within the social boundaries of the community. The increment in that proportion stemming from the individual's actual attendance at the ethnic church is not very large."[25] Ethnic associations encourage feelings of nationalism and are linked with an arousal of public interest in the ethnic group. The dominant role of religious institutions arises because of the number of activities and associations organized under their influence and support.[26]

After documenting the influence of institutional completeness on the direction of the social integration of the immigrant (whether he tends to become integrated within the "native" community, within his own ethnic community, or within a group of an ethnicity other than his own), Breton identifies three factors relating to the development of a public for ethnic organizations: (a) the possession of an attribute setting off the ethnic group from the native community (examples here are race, language, and religion), (b) the level of resources among the ethnic group members, and (c) the pattern of migration (the number and arrival rate of immigrants, as well as whether they arrive as individuals or as groups or as persons with prior ties to the ethnic community). Commenting on the second factor the author notes that in the case of an ethnic group of meager means there is an opportunity for the emergence of a "social entrepreneur" within the community "to organize something for the new immigrants in need, seeing there an interesting opportunity for himself" (for example, to increase membership in his church). Breton reports that "a strong positive relationship was in fact found between the proportion of manual workers in an ethnic group and the degree of institutional completeness of that group."[27]

Finally Breton observes that ethnic communities have a life-cycle. "The organizations established by these entrepreneurs will maintain themselves as long as a public exists to use their services, or as long as the ethnic identity of the organization is important for the members of the ethnic group. The very existence of such organizations . . . act[s] to strengthen this identity.[28] Ethnic organizations eventually disappear or lose their ethnic identity, with the passage of time and as assimilation into the native community occurs.

In summary to this point, while the religious orientations of rural blacks and rural blacks migrating to cities may have temporarily dampened political interests, at the same time they helped contribute to communalism; in the long run church development and political activity were melded. Urbanization and, especially, rising educational levels with the concomitant decrease in sectarianism, contributed to increasing militancy on the part of blacks.*

Parenthetically, it might be noted that in his recent book on resources available to black Americans for gaining power in the

*The term *sectarianism* here signifies an extreme religious conservatism or an otherworldly orientation, as contrasted to religious orthodoxy.

society, Coleman comments that social cohesion characterizing communities is "largely missing among blacks in America. . . . American communities, particularly in urban areas, have a generally low level of community cohesion; but this absence of cohesion is far more pronounced in black communities."[29] Coleman sees as important in the development of ethnic solidarity the growth of community groups, "some of them militant and organized as combat or confrontation groups, like the Black Panthers."[30] Yet Coleman fails to consider the presence of black churches and the existence of militant ministry styles such as that evinced by Albert Cleage of the Church of the Black Madonna in Detroit.[31] Religion is discussed by Coleman only under the concept of the Protestant ethic within his section on personal resources.

### Models of the Religion-Society Relationship

A survey of the salient concepts of the black church among sociologists and some social science-oriented theologians reveals three models for viewing the black church. Each has enjoyed a certain degree of validity in the context of a given time and place.

The first, or the assimilation-isolation model, is in some ways more complex than the others because its adherents have approached the church from two contradictory vantage points—from a position within the larger society and from the institutions of the black community itself. From the assimilation viewpoint, the level of participation in the church is relatively unimportant. Foremost in the thought of theorists of this position is the belief that there is an absolute necessity for the demise of the black church for the public good of the blacks. Events of the late 1950s and early 1960s seemed for a time to be conspiring with this viewpoint's ablest spokesman, E. Franklin Frazier, to enhance the popularity of such a model. Integration seemed the most desirable of all possible ends. Frazier commented that "integration for the majority of middle-class Negroes means the loss of racial identity or an escape from the lowly status of Negroes and the contempt of whites." As real integration seemed imminent, the black middle class removed or attempted to remove identifying names from their church organizations, such as the words "colored" or "African." Furthermore, there was a tendency to move away from the more traditional black denominations into the Presbyterian, Congregational, and Episcopal churches. Yet the religious life of the masses seemed relatively untouched by the new optimism prevailing elsewhere. "For the masses of Negroes," whatever its functions may have been as a compensatory or community-centered institution, the church had also been authoritarian and anti-intellectual. Frazier seemed to believe that with increasing assimilation it could not survive as a spiritual and social refuge for blacks of any class.[32]

The obverse or isolation aspect of this model stresses the social orientations which may contribute to the "isolation" of blacks from mainstream life. It focuses on the predominance of the lower statuses within the black community and the inverse correlation usually found between class and membership "involuntary isolation" by Orum. "Various forms of the prevalent social segregation of Negroes are viewed as conducive to the 'isolation' from civic affairs; this isolation, in turn, accounts for both a low level of participation in associations and a low voting turnout."[33] For an example of this orientation one can turn to Silberman's characterization of the black community as containing a "mass apathy [which] is too deeply rooted to be more than just temporarily pierced by a simple event ... or even a series of events."[34] Part of the isolation aspect of this model would be the description of black religion as lower-class, otherworldly, and acting as an opiate for problems of a temporal nature, including those calling for civil rights militancy.

The compensatory model for viewing the black church is in some degree a transitional state between the isolation-integration model and the ethnic community-prophetic model. St. Clair Drake and Horace Cayton may well have described this model most succinctly in their assessment of the power of the church in Chicago's South Side. They concluded that, while the church fulfilled different functions at various class levels, "it is probable, however, that the church's main attraction is the opportunity it gives for large masses of people to function in an organized group, to compete for prestige, to be elected to office, to exercise power and control, to win applause and acclaim."[35] The origin of this view of the church has, however, been most frequently connected with Gunnar Myrdal. In this connection, two points should be made. Myrdal did view the black community as essentially pathological and general developments of black culture as reactions to discrimination and segregation even when they were in a positive direction—as in the case of the development of racial pride. *"In practically all its divergences, American Negro culture is not something independent of general American culture. It is a distorted development, or a pathological condition, of the general American culture."*[36] Myrdal also made a specific application of this theory to black voluntary associations such as social clubs and civic improvement organizations (but not protest groups). He regarded activity in such associations as wasteful and merely an inferior substitute for the types of organizational life of mainstream society which were closed to black participation.[37] Although Myrdal did not make any such specific reference to the black church, it was, of course, a part of that "pathological" culture of the black community. Perhaps the most important factor in the way his work has been used is the assumption of his successors that the compensatory model was equally applicable to voluntary associations and to the churches.[38] Nicholas Babchuk and Ralph Thompson conducted a survey of the associational participation of blacks in Lincoln, Nebraska, in the spring of 1960. Although they did not include the church under the rubric of voluntary associations, they found that all those who belonged to at least one voluntary association also belonged to a church. While avoiding a direct equation of the church and the formal voluntary association, the authors concluded, "It is hard to deny . . . that the recognition that the Negro is able to obtain from his church and voluntary associations is almost impossible for him to obtain in any other sphere."[39]

Whether or not the compensatory model adequately fits the Myrdal work, it should be noted that there is a unique thrust to his specific comments on the church which also serves to place him in a position almost midway between the first and third models. The centrality of the research directed by Myrdal for post-World War II conceptions of race problems seems to justify a further examination of his observations. While accepting the goal of assimilation, he harbors a basically more positive attitude toward the black church. On the other hand, while Myrdal frequently stresses the importance of the church as a community center, he falls short of viewing the black church as prophetic and exhibiting a higher form of Christian commitment than does the white church.

Myrdal also departs from the Frazierian approach in seeing the church as a highly democratic institution. While acknowledging that as an instrument of social action the church has little ground for self-congratulation, Myrdal interprets its very existence as protest in its most obscure and latent form, especially where the pressure of caste is most severe: "Church and religion is a much needed front to give respectability and acceptability to the suppressed Negro protest. ... Sometime, somehow, the wrongs are going to be corrected and 'the last shall be first and the first shall be last.' There is not only consolation and escape in this religious teaching, but it also serves as a means of guarding the democratic faith in the minds of downtrodden black people."[40] Myrdal also lays great emphasis on the malleability of the church, the fact that it has been, in the past, what the black community wanted it to be, and that when the community demands a significant alteration in its stance, it will be forthcoming.[41] In stressing these aspects of the church, Myrdal comes very close to the ethnic community orientation. It may well be that only the particular time of his research and his status as a member of the white community prevented him from occupying a place in the third category.

Our third model emphasizes the importance of the black church as a base for building a sense of ethnic identity and a community of interest among its members. In addition, this model often accentuates the potential of the black church or minister as prophet to a corrupt white Christian nation. The Mays and Nicholson study of the black church, which falls into this category, emphasizes the "soul" of the church which outweighs such liabilities as "overchurching."[42] But in the decades following the appearance of their *Negro's Church* in 1933, few seemed so willing to overlook the current shortcomings of the church and to emphasize its potential greatness.[43] By the mid-1960s, however, as the earlier optimistic, nonviolent, black-and-white-together phase of the black revolution faded into history, some black theologians, while unhesitatingly condemning an old and accommodating black church, were once again eager to help realize a new black church which would be intimately involved in the cause of black people.

In 1971 the third model was given renewed credibility by Olsen, who drew upon the "ethnic community" thesis suggested by Lane and reviewed earlier in this introduction. Using 1967-1968 Indianapolis Area Project data, Olsen reported comparisons of black and white rates on fifteen dependent variables covering a wide variety of social and political activities. He controlled for socioeconomic status, and this resulted in a decrease of mean scores for whites, an increase for blacks. All coefficients were of low magnitude (many probably lacking significance) but positive in direction, indicating higher participation for blacks. (For example, the eta, or zero-order, coefficient for church participation was +.10, while the value of the beta, or partial, coefficient was +.18; the method of analysis by which these coefficients were determined will be introduced later in this study.) Black respondents who identified themselves as members of an ethnic minority scored higher than the nonidentifiers, giving credulity to the ethnic community model. Yet, analysis of additional data, collected in Detroit in 1957 before the civil rights and black power movements really began, already indicated the presence of this tendency for racial differences in participation to decline with the introduction of a control for socioeconomic status. Still, Indianapolis blacks were more likely to participate than whites (with the introduction of the control). Olsen concluded by accepting both the compensatory and ethnic community models as "partially valid."

It is undoubtedly true that many black people have been for a long time seeking to escape racial discriminations by forming and participating in their own voluntary associations. But it also seems almost self-evident that the recent emphasis on "black pride" and "black power" must certainly have stimulated many black persons to extend and intensify their participation in numerous realms of social and political life. In short, the compensation and ethnic community theses undoubtedly offer complementary, not contradictory, explanations of the tendency for blacks to participate more actively than whites of comparable socioeconomic and age levels in many social and political activities. Both processes could well be operating together on many blacks in this society, and both would tend to heighten their participation rates.[44]

Mays and Nicholson, writing in 1933, had even then noted the combined roles of the church in assisting the survival of black people through the comforts it offered and through the base it provided for the fight for racial justice (a base which was securely in black hands).[45] More recently, black theologians have emphasized the black church, not only as the power center of a self-aware black community, but as the prophet of Christian truth in a corrupt white society. The conversion of Joseph Washington, Jr., to a view of the black church as a potential maker of unity that will hold firm until equality has been won for all blacks[46] is the more striking for his earlier conviction that it was "the responsibility of all Negro congregations which exist essentially because of racial ties . . . to go out of business."[47]

Wilmore carried the commitment to the viability of the black church a step farther when he commented that the slogan of the Federal Council of Churches—A Non-segregated Church in a Non-segregated Society—"had become totally bankrupt as an expression of church action in the race field since its coinage in the 1930s.[48] The black church could perform a special service for American Christianity by reminding it of its revolutionary heritage from the Protestant Reformation and its neglected role of watchdog over secular culture.[49]

### Definitions of "Assimilation"

The assimilation-isolation model no longer seems pertinent in considering today's black religion if we mean by assimilation "a process in which persons of diverse ethnic and racial backgrounds come to interact, free of these constraints, in the life of the larger community . . . ; complete assimilation would mean that no separate social structures based on racial or ethnic concepts remained."[50] The change of heart exhibited by Joseph Washington testifies to the present day irrelevance of an assimilationist model in considering the black church.

Yet there is a related term that has not lost its relevance. "Acculturation" is the cultural change stemming from "the conjunction of two or more cultural systems or the transference of individuals . . . to new sociocultural environments."[51] Milton Gordon labels cultural integration into the majority society as "cultural assimilation," as distinct from "structural assimilation," or entrance into cliques and primary relationships (including churches) with the host society.[52] In terms of cultural assimilation, Gordon also differentiates between cultural traits that are "essential and vital ingredients of the group's cultural heritage" (intrinsic cultural traits or patterns) and those that are "external to the core of the group's ethnic cultural heritage" (extrinsic cultural traits or patterns). Among other examples, Gordon gives religious beliefs for the former and volatility of emotional expression for the latter.[53] The parallel here for a discussion of the acculturation of blacks in terms of their religious system is quite apparent; as blacks become more urbanized and have higher levels of education (presumably meaning a greater integration into American culture in general), certain extrinsic religious traits should diminish or even disappear, including rural religious emotionalism, while various intrinsic religious orientations (for example, the function of the church as an agency of protest) should remain and, if anything, become more pronounced.

### An Overview of This Study

The primary purpose of this study will be to assess the character of black religiosity as basically otherworldly and an opiate of civil rights militancy or as temporal and an inspiration of militancy. Because of the migration of blacks to cities (both southern and nonsouthern) and the increasing educational levels,[54] we may expect to find a tempering of the otherworldly religious orientation which probably was more characteristic of blacks than whites a half-century ago, when blacks were more likely to be rural, southern, and at lower educational levels. In other words, blacks have been culturally assimilated to a considerable degree and consequently they would increasingly expect their ministers to be "race men"—to work for the betterment of black conditions, especially in civil rights—and increasingly their religious involvement would be coupled with militancy rather than passivity.

Chapters 2 and 3 review previous studies of the black church. Of special interest will be the finding by Harry Richardson that where social conditions favored blacks (for example, where a high percentage of blacks owned rather than rented their farms), the black church was also strong. This testifies to the fact that the church received its strength not from isolationist feelings but from other sources.

In chapter 4 Gallup data will be used to compare the religious orientations of blacks and whites. Here a greater fealty to the church will be noted on the part of blacks, as measured by recency of attendance. This point will also be considered in the concluding chapter.

In chapter 5, again from secondary analyses of Gallup poll data, the subject of whether people believe that ministers should be involved in race protest will be considered. Here, desires by blacks and whites for the church's involvement or lack of involvement in social and political matters will be compared.

The direct relationship between religiosity, especially religious ideology, and militancy will be examined in the sixth chapter. The finding by Marx that "religion would seem to be an important factor working against the widespread radicalization of the Negro public" will be evaluated.[55] Religious ideology will be considered in terms of both sectarianism and orthodoxy. The former is more characteristic of an older orientation which is now diminishing because of acculturation. The latter, more characteristic of today's black Americans, is positively rather than inversely associated with militancy, a fact which suggests that today's black church and religiosity are not as oriented to the status quo as is generally believed.

In summary, the overall concern of this study is to assess the character of black religion as encouraging or dampening militancy. While it is probably true that on the whole blacks were more sectarian (or otherworldly) in their religious perspective than whites a half-century ago, with migration to the cities and with rising educational levels there is less reason to expect this racial differential to exist today. We might expect to find greater religious conservatism among blacks, but to anticipate a concomitant tendency to stress "pie in the sky by and by" rather than militancy in this-worldly matters seems unreasonable, when we consider that the black church is one of the major institutions of the black community and that today's black ideology is concerned with ending prejudice and discrimination as found in the majority society. There is little reason to expect a finding of greater sectarianism among blacks today, but, on the other hand, there is reason to expect greater loyalty to the church, as measured by church attendance, considering the major role of this institution in the black community. The religious institution can encourage political involvement because of the increased interaction of the members. Similarly, the presence of the church has meant a greater degree of institutional completeness in the black community. As assimilation appeared to be occurring in the mid-1960s, attendance rates could have been depressed and as it became apparent that the assimilation model was undermined by the lack of structural assimilation, the black church could have begun a period of revival as measured by attendance figures.[56] Trend attendance figures will be presented in the concluding chapter in order to assess this relationship between the black church and the larger, majority society.

# 2:

## The Black Church
## before World War I

It seems clear that any examination of modern black urban adjustment and of the role of the black church in an era of black consciousness requires some background knowledge of the pre-Emancipation black church. The Afro-American church of slave times was neither monolithic nor noncontroversial. The religious life of the isolated plantation slave, whether carried on clandestinely or with the open encouragement of the master, was far removed from the sophisticated, institutionalized Christianity of the independent black church communities of the urban, free North. Many scholars who are currently in the forefront of the new black theology have engaged in the continuing controversy over the presence of Africanisms in the religious life of the slaves and the potential for protest and revolution evident in the early black church. While it is virtually impossible to attempt estimates of the proportions of protest or escapist thought in antebellum black religion or to reject or accept wholeheartedly the arguments for the survival of African beliefs in Christian rites of worship, existing studies do give some idea of the complex nature of the black church as it matured during the first centuries of its existence and of what intellectual and spiritual accouterments it would bring (or fail to bring) to the service of the freedmen.

Without delving into the motivations of the slave in adopting Christianity, it seems clear that, for many, access to Christianity was controlled by whites. Hostility toward the Christianizing of the slave could be found among the seventeenth-century slaveholders who feared that Christian baptism might give the black a legitimate claim to freedom. Even when this fear had been dispelled, not all whites were blessed with the sort of proselytizing piety which would deprive them of rest until they had provided for the spiritual welfare of their chattels. Among those whites who were so blessed, many had the additional prodding of the belief that Christianizing would make the slave more docile, more honest, more willing to fulfill his duty as servant to his earthly master. There also seems to be little doubt that most masters realized that Christianity must be properly edited for slaves, that the ability to read the Bible and the privilege of preaching the Word were best reserved for the white race. When the white guard slipped and slaves began to read the Bible or black preachers were allowed to tend their own slave flocks, the fear of abolitionist tracts and of the Denmark Veseys and Nat Turners of the South would usually bring the whites to their senses. While covert prayer meetings were surely conducted, it does seem that the plantation slave's religious life was probably that most effectively controlled by whites.

Worship for the plantation slave took a variety of forms. Sometimes the master allowed the slave preacher to conduct services as long as a white in authority was present.[1] In areas where holdings in land and slaves were smaller, both races might attend church together (with the blacks segregated in the gallery or to the rear). If the plantation were large the planter might provide his own church and hire a cleric, or he might simply rely on itinerant preachers to provide occasional inspiration.[2] Other masters considered the slaves' religious instruction their personal responsibility. But the black congregation of any substantial autonomy seems to have been a comparative rarity in this setting.[3]

Richard Wade has suggested that the very dimensions of the problem of providing religion to large concentrations of slaves in the Southern cities hampered whites' initiative and frequently left them in methodological debates while blacks attended to their own religious organization.[4] The disparity between what the law allowed and what the blacks, slave and free, were able to achieve suggests the importance of the urban antebellum church in the South as a training ground for future leaders. "Of course, formally the law vested supervision and control in white leaders, but the fundamental tasks—recruiting members, finding and supporting ministers, paying rents, and staffing the Sunday Schools—fell to the blacks themselves. If this activity had been left to regular denominations, the churches would have scarcely survived, much less flourished."[5] While independent, formal black churches could be found throughout the major cities of the South, scholars continually note the intriguing case of Charleston, where the church and revolution seemed to go hand in hand. The creation of a separate African church, not attended by whites, shortly before the Denmark Vesey plot of 1822 led many whites to assume a connection.[6] In spite of continued apprehensiveness among white Charlestonians, blacks continued to extend their church membership. As Wade notes, one of the most important functions of the church was its ability to impart some sense of dignity and worth to the members of a lower caste— nowhere more so than in the funerals, which insured that "the body would not be disposed of like that of a dead animal but the book be closed with some dignity and solemnity."[7]

But even more than in the urban South it was in the urban, antebellum North that the patterns of separatism and independence which would characterize the postbellum black church were set. Certain groups in the North, most notably the Puritans, Anglicans (through the Society for the Propagation of the Gospel), and Quakers, had from the beginning displayed an ample concern for the spiritual welfare of the blacks. Especially in the eighteenth century there was rather spirited competition among the Quakers, Puritans, and Anglicans for black souls.[8] Nevertheless, Lorenzo Greene, whose study of the Negro in colonial New England remains a classic, believes that the majority of blacks in New England as elsewhere remained unconverted.[9] The event which would herald a new era in church development among northern black people would not occur until the American Revolution had been won and white America had begun to turn its attention to nation-building.

Winthrop Jordan's recent study in American racism, *White over Black: American Attitudes toward the Negro, 1550-1818,* contains perhaps the most perceptive narrative of the beginning of the independent black church movement. In a direct confrontation between national racism and Christian equality, the forces of racism triumphed. The momentous break with the predominant pattern came in 1787, when the black members of St. George's Methodist Church in Philadelphia, led by Richard Allen and Absalom Jones, were shunted from their regular places to seats around the wall and, finally, to the gallery. Even this did not satisfy the whites, however, and one of the white churchmen attempted to move Absalom Jones even further back in the gallery while Jones was kneeling in prayer. This act proved to be the last straw for the blacks, who had recently made substantial contributions to the remodeling of the church, and they walked out en masse. At first Allen and Jones formed a Free African Society with a Quaker-like orientation. However, the pair soon left this group to form the first Negro Episcopal Church (under Jones's leadership) and the African Methodist Episcopal Church (with Allen as its first bishop). As Jordan noted, the whites seemed to find the building of these separate churches nearly as pleasing as the blacks did, and he notes that by the 1790s this trend was well established.[10] Independent black churches proliferated. According to Litwack, "By 1830, the Negro church movement reflected much of the chaos and multiplicity of sects that prevailed among the whites."[11] While the Baptists attracted even more substantial numbers of free blacks than the Methodists, the Methodist church was best able to carve out a network of black congregations that, though scattered throughout the North, could exert some sustained influence on their members' behalf.[12]

Just as many of the forms taken by the black church in its early years would provide the models for church development in the postwar era, so would many of the attractions which Christianity held for the slave continue to appeal to an oppressed people after their nominal emancipation. In what is still a compelling and balanced interpretation of the antebellum development of the church, W. E. B. Du Bois assembled a developmental model which half a century of critics have remodeled but never yet entirely razed. While in no sense underestimating the shattering effects upon the African of transportation and enforced labor in an alien culture, Du Bois argues that some traces of communal life were retained. "The chief remaining institution was the priest or medicine man. He early appeared on the plantation and found his function as the healer of the sick, the interpreter of the unknown, the comforter of the sorrowing, the supernatural avenger of wrong, and the one who rudely but picturesquely expressed the longing, disappointment, and resentment of a stolen and oppressed people. Thus, as bard, physician, judge, and priest, within the narrow limits allowed by the slave system, rose the Negro preacher and under him the first Afro-American institution, the Negro church."[13] While the church under this early half-African leader was as much a representative of voodooism as of Christianity, with the passing of generations the church became Christian. Du Bois found it especially significant that the faith of the Baptists and Methodists spread most rapidly among the slaves and that "as a social institution [the church] antedated by many decades the monogamic Negro home." It was its strength as a social institution, particularly, that led Du Bois to view the church as "peculiarly the expression of the inner ethical life of the people who compose it." Accepting as he did the idea that the blacks were indeed singularly religious and inclined toward the supernatural, he saw that the enslaved viewed their plight as the triumph of evil over them. At first the slave called upon aids offered by his old religion—everything from witchcraft to blood sacrifice. But as these continually failed to bring redemption to the slave in the American South, his will to resist faded and he found in the "passive submission embodied in the newly learned Christianity" a philosophy of life more attuned to his needs. Du Bois also believed that this fatalism often degenerated, in the morally lax plantation atmosphere, into "a philosophy of indulgence and crime" which plagued many blacks long after emancipation.[14] But instead of assuming that the enslaved blacks of the antebellum South had no viable black role models, Du Bois points to the free blacks of the North where the spirit of revolt still lived. Du Bois displays an understandable ambivalence toward what became a transfixing religion of freedom:

> For fifty years Negro religion thus transformed itself and identified itself with the dream of abolition, until that which was a radical fad in the white North and an anarchistic plot in the white South had become a religion to the black world. Thus, when emancipation finally came, it seemed to the freedman a literal coming of the Lord. His fervid imagination was stirred as never before, by the tramp of armies, the blood and dust of battle, and the wail and whirl of social upheaval. He stood dumb and motionless before the whirlwind: what had he

to do with it? Was it not the Lord's doing, and marvellous in his eyes? Joyed and bewildered with what came, he stood awaiting new wonders till the inevitable age of reaction swept over the nation and brought the crisis of today.[15]

Africanisms, accommodations to the new world situation, social protest and otherworldly withdrawal, a continuity in leadership, and a sometimes paralyzing faith were all elements which Du Bois placed within the frame of the slaves' religious experience. Some forty years later, Melville Herskovits would attempt to redefine the relative importance of the various elements. For Herskovits, any assumption that the slaves gravitated to the Baptists more than to other Christian sects because their simple services appealed to the "simple" slave was of questionable accuracy. Neither the well-known "democracy" of the Baptist faith nor the relative straightforwardness of its service was a sufficient explanation of its popularity among the transplanted Africans. Rather: "In the New World, where the aggressive proselytizing activities of Protestantism made the retention of the inner forms of African religion as difficult as its outer manifestations, the most logical adaptation for the slaves to make to the new situation, and the simplest, was to give their adherence to that Christian sect which in its ritualism most resembled the types of worship known to them."[16]

Herskovits thus essentially denies that the African slave in the new World required anything more in the way of either revolutionary spirit or comfort from his religion than he ever had in his homeland. E. Franklin Frazier, who denounced the Herskovits argument as misguided, offered a reformulation of the elements of slave religion which would go relatively unchallenged until the 1960s. Frazier believed that the process of dehumanization which the black people endured, from the moment when they were herded into barracoons to await transportation, through the horrors of the "middle passage," and the final seasoning in America in which masters united to discourage the retention of any segment of African heritage, did effectively destroy their old base of "social cohesion." He thus regards it as "impossible to establish any continuity between African religious practices and the Negro church in the United States."[17] Frazier agrees that the Methodists and Baptists were particularly successful in their proselyting activities among blacks, but he attributes this to their emphasis on religious feeling, and he notes that "in the emotionalism of the camp meetings and revivals some social solidarity, even if temporary, was achieved, and [slaves] were drawn into a union with their fellow men." Further, as the black participated in Christian services, he was drawn out of his "moral isolation in the white man's world."[18] The Bible, as it was transmitted to the slave, provided him with a "new theology." The clue as to the direction in which the slave adapted his new religion to his needs may be found, according to Frazier, in his spirituals, which are predominantly religious and otherworldly in content. So important was the spiritual uplift and sense of fellowship provided by Christian worship that the Negro church among the slaves became the "invisible institution" in which the black preacher was perhaps the most clearly recognized bulwark. But Frazier acknowledges that his powers were always circumscribed, not only by the degree of influence he could sustain over his congregation but by the latitude allowed him by the white power structure.[19]

Frazier's concept of slave religion was that it was unremittingly compensatory. While Vincent Harding agrees that much of slave religion undoubtedly fit this mold, he asserts the "ambiguity" of black religion. In the case of the Denmark Vesey plot of 1822, rebellion had become part of the fabric of church life for the black Charlestonians of the African Church. "The agitation from 1815 to 1818 and the concerted withdrawal from the white congregations in the latter year took significant courage for the slaves. The raising of an independent house of worship . . . was clearly an act of defiance for the world to see. . . . It is, then, essential to note that the sense of black solidarity was imbedded in the organization of the Negro church."[20]

On an individual level Nat Turner, the "Jesus of Southampton," most vividly embodied the religion of black rebellion. But Harding suggests that those men and women who committed suicide to reach their otherworldly rewards, who rejected the submissiveness in white-edited Christianity, who, while strong in their faith, seized every opportunity to flee North from slavery to a better world in the here and now, were also expressing resistance. Harding likewise views the spirituals as musical expressions of the ambiguity inherent in slave religion, transporting some blacks "beyond the earth entirely," while filling others "with a sense of God's awesome calling for their present moment."[21]

*Reconstruction to World War I*

With the end of the Civil War millions of freedmen found themselves cut loose from the only style of life, undesirable as it was, that they had ever known and suddenly called upon to create their own institutions and communities. Constantly harried in their struggles by the venom of white racists North and South and disappointed by the frailties of better-meaning whites who could not sustain their commitment to blacks once such commitment had gone out of style, the freedmen built their new lives. At the center of their efforts to gain an education, to build a family structure which would conform to white American culture, and to develop community leaders capable of fighting for the race stood the black church. The traditional views of E. Franklin Frazier which portrayed the church of this period as a rank accommodator, run by men of strong personalities whose primary interest was the maintenance of personal power, are now in sharp dispute. Studies such as Jon Butler made in St. Paul have raised anew questions about the power of individual preachers, the ties between politics and religion, and the role of the church in the black community.[22] The work of S. P. Fullinwider[23] has renewed our awareness of the militancy of the racial Christianity of the period which informed Carter Woodson's early study of the black church.[24] It was, all in all, an extraordinarily complex period in the development of the black church. The demands of the black community were so great that the many failures of the church are more readily detectable than the triumphs, often small but nevertheless real, which were so persistently fought for.

*Emerging Structural Patterns in the Postwar Church*

As E. Franklin Frazier has said, the Civil War brought a uniting of the institutional church which had already grown up among the free blacks, North and South, with the "invisible church" which had served the slave.[25] Although trained leaders were few—and during the early years of Reconstruction the more talented of the black community often turned to politics rather than the church—varied church organizations were gradually carved out by the blacks. Carter Woodson has presented a detailed picture of how the new black churches evolved among the Methodists and Baptists, the two denominations which would continue to have the greatest appeal for the masses. The independent African Methodists were now freer to proselyte in the South as well as the North; in addition, the fact that black men occupied the highest church offices exerted tremendous appeal. Nevertheless, many black Methodists in the North continued to give their loyalty to the Methodist Episcopal Church, North, which increasingly tried to accommodate the desire of its black members that black congregations be assigned black pastors. In 1866 it also provided for an annual conference of black ministers, something for which the black members had been agitating since 1844. The Methodist Episcopal Church, South, however, for whatever reason, more readily granted its black members autonomy by agreeing to the creation of the Colored Methodist Episcopal Church. Woodson notes that the motivations of the whites in ridding themselves so quickly of the black members continue to be in question and that some blacks went so far as to suspect that the C.M.E. church was somehow designed to lead the blacks back into slavery.[26]

The Baptists, however, would enjoy an even greater vogue, for the democratic nature of the Baptist organization which had been so attractive before emancipation now lured an inordinate number of black men to the ministry. Although many eagerly set about gathering their followers and building churches, others were temporarily sidetracked into Reconstruction politics and would turn to the church only after other avenues for their ambitions had been closed.[27]

In spite of the lack of the type of national organization which characterized the Methodists, many Baptist congregations formed themselves into associations for mutual aid. Meetings of these associations gave many Baptists contacts with racial goals and white opinion which they might not otherwise have had. "In those meetings the uniformed heard of the urgent need to educate the masses, the duty of the ministry to elevate the laity, and the call upon all to Christianize the heathen. The periodical visits of white churchmen, interested either in the Negro or in exploiting them, brought new light as to what was going on in the other bodies conducted by men of higher attainments."[28] The Baptists did begin organizing themselves into state conventions as early as 1866, however, and from that into more national bodies. They also tended to retain what they could from the white Baptists—including their literature—and they welcomed the missionaries sent by the northern Baptists.[29]

These immediate, postwar attempts at organization, while successful in their way, cannot be construed as a final settlement. During the period roughly coinciding with the years in which Reconstruction was formally abandoned, a battle began between the conservatives and progressives within the black church which would run to the end of the century and beyond.[30] Like the membership, the battles seemed to have centered in the Methodist Episcopal Church and among the Baptists. While at first the conflict seemed to be one of age, with the progressive young pitted against their conservative elders, in time the split became ideological, cutting across age lines. Education appears to have been at the root of the rift, for even brief exposure to education tended to make the intelligent young less than satisfied with the "old-time" religion. "Religion to the progressives became a Christian experience rather than the wild notions of revelation."[31] The progressives also realized that religion without education could not successfully uplift the race. The conservatives viewed the new group as a threat to the church, for they continued to believe that the individual existed for the glory of the church rather than the church for the benefit of the individual. The progressives often suspected the conservatives of questionable morals, and even of graft, in building a money-oriented church. The conservatives, on the other hand, refused to overlook the small vices that growing sophistication made desirable to the progressives, and staunchly opposed changes in the services which might give them a more intellectual tone. As progressives found themselves suspect and powerless in their old churches, many left to join the more hospitable Congregationalists, Presbyterians, Episcopalians, and Catholics. Within the more flexible Baptist churches, some progressives formed their own schismatic congregations.

But agitation against the black conservatives rather soon expanded into something of a black separatist movement. Progressive agitation for separation from the Methodist Episcopal Church was eventually quelled as whites made further concessions to black members. But the independence movement in the Baptist fellowship led to the formation of the National Baptist Convention in 1886. From Woodson's viewpoint, in an era when blacks were increasingly thrown back on their own resources, the independent black churches were strides ahead in learning to care for themselves. The success of these churches could be seen most plainly in the special religious census of 1906 which showed all-black denominations as having 87 percent of the total black membership.[32]

In summary, it can perhaps be said that the early response of the church to emancipation was to organize itself as rapidly as possible through the most readily available means. As differentiation occurred within the black community and as the realities of white hostility and its meaning for the church as well as for the black community became clear, the churches gradually re-formed themselves along lines which made them more responsive to the needs of the race and of individual blacks. Still, the trend toward membership in all-black denominations did not automatically equip the black church to face the technical, urbanized world of the twentieth century.

*Functions of and Challenges to the Postwar Church*

E. Franklin Frazier, who has argued that slavery totally demolished the old communal and family ties, sees the black church as providing the initial means for organizing the life of the black community into a stratified system.[33] Although there was some differentiation among the slaves based on the role they occupied in the plantation economy, with freedom and the merging of the "invisible church" with the organized churches which had grown up among blacks before the war, a new basis of stratification was formed. Frazier argues that many of the antebellum free blacks, both mulattoes and pure blacks, had adapted to European culture to a greater extent than the enslaved. As a free and mulatto ancestry became the mark of social distinction in the postwar world, it was also closely reflected in the denominational affiliation of the black people. While the masses were concentrated in the Methodist and Baptist denom-

inations, there was often separation of churches by color.[34]
The fine gradations which could distinguish one church from
another can be seen in W. E. B. Du Bois's description of the
membership of the various black churches of Philadelphia at the turn
of the century:

> Without wholly conscious effort the Negro church has become
> a centre of social intercourse to a degree unknown in white
> churches even in the country. The various churches, too,
> represent social classes. At St. Thomas' [Protestant Episcopal]
> one looks for the well-to-do Philadelphians, largely descen-
> dants of favorite mulatto house servants, and consequently
> well-bred and educated, but rather cold and reserved to
> strangers and newcomers; at Central Presbyterian one sees the
> older, simpler set of respectable Philadelphians with distinctly
> Quaker characteristics—pleasant but conservative; at Bethel
> [Methodist] may be seen the best of the great laboring class—
> steady, honest people, well dressed and well fed, with church
> and family traditions; at Wesley [Methodist] will be found the
> new arrivals, the sight-seers and the strangers to the city—
> hearty and easy-going people, who welcome all comers and ask
> few questions; at Union Baptist one may look for the Virginia
> servant girls and their young men; and so on throughout the
> city. Each church forms its own social circle, and not many
> stray beyond its bounds.[35]

Both Du Bois and Frazier suggest the inclusiveness of the black
church—the entire population seems to have been divided into neat
parcels which have been distributed among the rival denominations.
But at least one recent work, Jon Butler's study of the black church
in St. Paul, Minnesota, from 1860 to 1900, has raised doubts about
the congruency of the black church and the black community.
Butler found, for instance, that "the ratios of female to male
members in these congregations was the reverse of the sex ratio in
the adult population." He notes that St. Paul was unusual in having a
predominance of males in the black population, but he stresses the
unrepresentativeness of the church organizations.[36] The fact that
the black churches of St. Paul did not seem to minister to the needs
of single black males, raises some serious questions about other
functions of the church which will be discussed later.

E. Franklin Frazier has also linked the black church to the formation of a "monogamous and stable family life" out of the presumably chaotic conditions of the slave world. The Bible supported patriarchal authority, and substantial numbers of the new leaders in building black community life were also preachers.[37] Although Frazier's strong man interpretation is questionable, such diverse critics of the church as W. E. B. Du Bois and Booker T. Washington have dwelt on the moral leadership role of the black church. Du Bois, in studying Philadelphia, noted that the congregations, and not the ministers, set the moral tone. "There has been a slow working toward a literal obeying of the puritan and ascetic standard of morals which Methodism imposed on the freedmen; but condition and temperament have modified these. The grosser forms of immorality, together with theatre-going and dancing, are specifically denounced; nevertheless, the precepts against specific amusements are often violated by church members."[38] And although the standards may have been lower than desirable, Du Bois credits the churches with effectively deterring offenders. Washington urged that the black church should develop a "more definite connection with the social and moral life of the Negro people. Could this connection be effected in a large degree, it would give to the movement for the upbuilding of the race the force and inspiration of a religious motive."[39]

*Education*

The church's relationship to education is considerably more difficult to pin down. In the early Reconstruction era, such predominantly white denominations as the Baptists, Methodists, Presbyterians, Congregationalists, and Society of Friends initiated the establishment of schools for the freedmen. Working in tandem with such groups as the federal Freedmen's Bureau and the American Freedmen's Aid Commission, the denominations helped to impart a religious flavor to the initial educational experiences of the freedmen.[40] The existing black churches were, however, equally eager to aid in this grand educational effort "as a means to spread the gospel through an intelligent ministry and to enable the laity to appreciate it as the great leverage in the uplift of the man far down."[41] Woodson cites such undertakings as the establishment of Union Seminary near Columbus, Ohio (later merged with the Methodist-sponsored Wilberforce), Morris Brown in Atlanta, Livingstone College in Salisbury, North Carolina. But the influence of the Northern white denominations on black education at this time was overwhelming, and Woodson observes that it was fortunate indeed that these churches opted for education rather than for proselyting in their quest for the souls of the freedmen.[42] As early as 1875 results of this educational crusade were visible in the black church itself. If August Meier's findings of a correlation between limited training/conservatism and professional training/radicalism of the clergy are correct, the educational system begun in the late 1860s would influence the character and militancy of the church well into the next century.[43]

The relationship between education and religion was clearly a reciprocal one. Even E. Franklin Frazier, who consistently ignores the more militant and intellectual trends within the black church and comes down hard on the anti-intellectualism of the black preacher, notes the contributions of the church toward public schooling. The black churches through such homely devices as church suppers raised millions of dollars for the schools aided by the Rosenwald Fund.[44]

### The Church and Economics

The black church's impact on the economic well-being of the black community is a many-faceted and often controversial subject. The church may be considered, according to different points of view, as a training center in corporate economics, or as a parasite drawing off the life-blood of a deprived people into unnecessary buildings and bloated salaries for sweet-talking preachers. At least in this period, it does seem that the experience gained in raising money for churches provided some valuable business experience for a people who were ordinarily shut out from the entrepreneurial side of the business relationship.

Among the more important economic offshoots of the churches were the mutual aid societies, the earliest of which was the Free African Society of Absalom Jones and Richard Allen of Philadelphia. These societies were designed to provide assistance during sickness and to help widows and their children. After the war these societies continued to be formed, and Frazier notes that six of the nine beneficial societies formed in Atlanta between the end of the Civil War and 1898 were connected with the churches.[45] The "sickness and burial" societies formed among rural freedmen also show this close tie between religion and economic cooperation. As Frazier notes, "The important fact . . . is that these benevolent societies grew out of the Negro church and were inspired by the spirit of Christian charity. They were supported by the pennies which the Negroes could scrape together in order to aid each other in time of sickness but more especially to insure themselves a decent Christian burial."[46]

In addition, some fraternal orders established by black ministers could provide more adventurous enterprises. Frazier cites the Reverend Washington Browne's Grand United Order of the True Reformers, which began in 1876, as the Grand Fountain of True Reformers, with 2,000 members. The True Reformers tried their hands at a weekly paper, real estate brokerage, banking, the hotel business, a building and loan association, and retail merchandising, among other business ventures.[47]

While Du Bois's intensive survey of the black churches of Philadelphia in 1897 gave an idea of how the visible wealth of the black community seemed to be concentrated in the churches,[48] Gilbert Osofsky's study of Harlem suggests how the wealthiest of the black churches could significantly affect the movement of an urban population:

> But the Negro churches did more than simply follow their members to Harlem. Many were able to realize large profits by selling property in the midtown area at high prices and moving uptown where land and property had depreciated in value before World War I. The more important and wealthy congregations not only built new churches in Harlem, but invested heavily in local real estate. Negro churches became the largest Negro property owners in Harlem. St. Mark's Methodist Episcopal, Abyssinian Baptist, and "Mother Zion" owned houses in Harlem prior to 1915. After the war, they and other Negro churches continued to invest heavily in land and homes. Some

of the houses purchased by churches were on blocks covered by restrictive covenants, but nothing could be done to prevent such transactions. By becoming landholders, Negro churches helped transform Harlem to a Negro section.[49]

The most aggressive and the wealthiest of these churches was the fashionable St. Philip's Protestant Episcopal Church, whose light-skinned minister bought land from unsuspecting whites who believed they were keeping their real estate out of the hands of Negroes. In 1911 St. Philip's moved into its new quarters in Harlem and was able to use the impressive sums realized from the sale of its Tenderloin property to purchase apartment houses which would, for the first time, receive black tenants.[50]

### The Church, Politics, and the Changing Minister

In the immediate postbellum years, the black minister was especially susceptible to the excitement of politics. While, as Carter Woodson has suggested, some may have been motivated by a "desire to attain positions of prominence in keeping with the traditions of the white people of the South," Woodson is also correct in pointing to a very real need for leadership in a variety of areas where none had existed prior to Emancipation.[51] When for at least a limited time, political office became a realistic goal for talented blacks, it is not too surprising that the preachers, as the only group of leaders acceptable even in slave times, should have expanded their horizons. Some left the ministry altogether, others tried to combine politics and a church career, while a still larger number used their pulpits to politicize their congregations but did not themselves actively seek office. Although some, notably in the North, managed to continue this way of life for a few years after the end of Reconstruction, southern ministers quickly found themselves once again tethered to their churches.[52]

During the last decades of the nineteenth century and the opening one of the twentieth, the churches and their ministers gradually settled into a routine of erecting buildings and turning their churches into the kind of community social and literary centers described by Du Bois in *The Philadelphia Negro*. Again, there were exceptions, as the case of St. Paul suggests. Butler found that while congregations and churches as institutions took virtually no part in local political activity, nearly all politically active blacks were members of churches. As he notes, "Negro political organizations were composed largely of congregational members and tended toward a collective of some of the ministers and most of the important lay leaders in the congregations."[53] Both Du Bois's Philadelphia study and Osofsky's analysis of Harlem indicate that even in northern cities the political activism of the St. Paul blacks was unusual.

Recent studies by August Meier and S. P. Fullinwider have brought into focus the social and intellectual characteristics of the conservative clergy as well as of the fewer but highly influential militant clerics of the early 1900s. Meier found that most of the important men in the A.M.E. church, the A.M.E. Zion church, the C.M.E. church, and the National Baptist Convention were conservatives. Most had been born slaves and had no professional or higher education. "In general they enunciated a gradualist philosophy of self-help, racial solidarity, and economic progress as the keys to citizenship rights." In varying degrees they interlarded their exhortations to attain the Bookerite goals of self-help and earned friendship and respect from southern whites with pleas for political rights and an end to segregation. Although some of them had political experience or hopes, they generally lined up with Booker T. Washington and "soft-pedaled the importance of political participation."[54]

The leaders of the mass churches were not uniformly conservative, and Meier notes that a growing militancy is apparent in the records of their quadrennial conferences. At the 1912 meetings, detectably more militant than those of 1900, the noted radical Reverdy Ransom was elected editor of the A.M.E. *Review*. Although he lacks data on the congregations, Meier suspects that among the mass churches the scattered militants were pastors of the more elite congregations. But it was "among the more elite Presbyterian, Congregational, and Episcopal churches of the Northern and border states that the protest point of view found its chief strength."[55] Meier notes the case of Francis Grimke, pastor of a fashionable Washington, D. C., Presbyterian church and a noted intellectual. In the 1890s Grimke was numbered among staunch backers of Washington, but by 1903 he had clearly joined the opposition in his support of full citizenship rights for blacks. Meier concludes that "broadly speaking the ministers exhibited the same range of ideologies as other leaders, with a strong sentiment in favor of Washington among them, especially among those who were leaders in the mass churches."[56]

S. P. Fullinwider, while basically accepting Meier's characterization of the clergy as fundamentally conservative with a handful of aggressive and influential militants, has illuminated the rationales which enabled the two disparate types to function in the post-Reconstruction world. The conservative black minister had to reconcile two contradictory images of his people—first the view of the Negro as inferior and in need of the help of white men of good will, and second, the image of the black man as Christ-like. Fullinwider suggests that it "was their great faith that God is operating the world according to some great plan" that enabled them to live with the contradictory images of the white and black. On the one hand, God may have brought the African to America to enable him to become Christian—or, on the other, he might have been sent so that the white man could learn "true Christian Leadership."[57]

Yet in the late 1880s and 1890s a trend away from confidence in the white man and a questioning of orthodoxy becomes barely visible. But these early dissenters were timid, and it took an R. R. Wright, Jr., and a Reverdy Ransom to light the fires in the militant camp.[58] Ransom and Wright began their battles against orthodoxy when they struggled for the life of the Institutional Church and Social Settlement, which they started in 1900, modeling it after Jane Addams's Hull House. Both, as the years passed, became caught in a new kind of tension—between aggression and black racism on one side and Christianity and a gospel of love on the other.[59] As Fullinwider suggests, the thought developed by these two militants would have an effect far beyond the church itself:

> Ransom and Wright had taken the Christ-like image of the Negro, had added a mission ideology, and made it the core of their religion. Their religion had an important influence in the councils of the Niagara Movement and the early NAACP; it penetrated the classrooms of the Negro universities and colleges, became sociological dogma taught to thousands of students from the turn of the century through the 1920's. It represented the transformation of the old slave religion into a

religion of militancy—the overthrow of the slave psychology. As such, it was a step in the emancipation of the Negro mind. But it had channeled aggression into the realm of mythology and so was itself an intellectual prison. It was a strange brew: part Social Gospel in its emphasis on the brotherhood of man, part racism. It set the Negro up as the moral arbiter of American civilization.[60]

# 3:

# The Great Migration to the
# Beginning of the Civil
# Rights Movement

With World War I came the beginning of the great migration to the North, stimulated by a variety of converging factors. Low wages and the devastation caused by the boll weevil and floods in the years 1914 to 1916 suddenly made economic conditions in the South more unbearable than usual. The sharp decline of foreign immigration after 1914 and the heightened demands of industry provided a severe labor shortage in the North. The perennial social conditions of the South, combined with the cajoling voices of the Negro press and the labor recruiter, did much to break down any barriers. Long after the jobs had evaporated and many had found the North as inhospitable in its way as the South they had left behind, the stream of black migrants continued to flow north.[1] Not surprisingly, the central institution of black community life was confronted with a generally unanticipated challenge which would alter its nature considerably. Not only would the urban church of the North have to make unprecedented accommodations, but the rural church of the South, which had seemed to have such a stable membership base, would suddenly have to re-form its ranks in the face of dwindling resources in membership, finances, and leadership.

During the decades of the twenties, thirties, and forties, black social scientists and their white colleagues initiated a number of studies of the church, of the reformation it had undergone, of the alterations in policy which would be necessary if it were to meet successfully the enormous demands made upon it in this new era. Many dedicated researchers, with varying degrees of sympathy for the institution itself, sought to make the black leadership more aware of the limitations and possibilities of the church so that they might strengthen it to fulfill its new role in black community life or else make enlightened decisions to turn elsewhere should the church prove unadaptable. Whether black leadership actively utilized the findings of these researchers is debatable even now, but their efforts have made this era one of the best understood of all periods in the development of an institution as complex as the black church.

### The Church They Left Behind

The ice-breaking research in the rural church seems to have come from the study undertaken by Benjamin E. Mays and Joseph W. Nicholson for the Institute of Social and Religious Research which resulted in the volume *The Negro's Church,* published in 1933. Although the Mays and Nicholson study had a decidedly urban focus (609 urban churches in twelve cities were studied, compared with 185 rural churches in four nonurban regions), it provided valuable statistics and suggested some of the problem areas in rural church life. Although more than half of the black population could still be found in rural areas in the South (the rural population of the North was negligible), the rural areas had suffered notable losses since 1910. The black urban population had increased by approximately 875,000 between 1910 and 1920, while from 1920 to 1930, the rural South lost 650,000 blacks to southern cities and 450,000 to northern cities. Although the effects of migration had been less severe among the rural churches studied than the researchers had anticipated, socioeconomic changes within the resident population were adversely affecting the churches. Fully 73.5 percent of the 185 rural churches had memberships of less than 200, compared to 35.6 percent of the 609 urban churches. Further, according to statistics of the *Federal Census of Religious Bodies,* the average expenditure per member for all urban black churches in 1926 was $12.42, while for the rural member it was only $6.14. Of the churches studied, however, Mays and Nicholson found that in 1930, the rural churches expended only $3.00 per member. In analyzing the occupations of country residents, it was found that the number of black landowners was declining even more rapidly than the number of renters and sharecroppers. The high percentage of the more migratory renters and croppers increased the instability of the membership, making this "possibly the most complicated problem confronting the rural church."[2]

Nor were the only problems to be found among the members; Mays and Nicholson found little to encourage them in their analysis of the rural clergy. Fully 96 percent of the clergy of the rural churches studied had less than a college or a seminary education. These clergymen also tended to be older than their urban counterparts. They exhibited a high turnover rate and were frequently preachers only, rather than pastors to their flocks. The fact that the churches could pay only small salaries, and that the rural minister tended to serve multiple churches, did not augur well for improvements in an undesirable situation. Under the circumstances revealed in their study, Mays and Nicholson stressed that "if these churches do not consolidate, a large number of them will die of natural causes." But the church of an impoverished people could not in itself reverse current conditions in the rural South, and the authors were quick to recognize this. "It is the conviction of the authors that healthier days include the working out of a farm system by agricultural experts, encouraged and aided by the Federal Government, so that life on the farm will be made attractive, safe, and profitable for the Negro. They include a more vigorous program to improve the inadequate educational system under which most rural Negroes still live, and certainly a more humane treatment of him on the part of those who are intrusted with the task of administering the law."[3]

Although Mays and Nicholson had touched on the inadequacy of the Sunday school program and the youth program in particular,[4] it was Charles Johnson who would fathom the depths of youthful alienation in the rural black church. Johnson found that the church had altered little since its early postslavery days, that it was the school which was responsible for introducing new values into the community. "It is an inescapable observation that the rural Negro church is a conservative institution, preserving in large part many values which, in the general cultural ferment of the Negro group, might well be altered. Its greatest present value appears to be that of providing emotional relief for the fixed problems of a hard life."[5] Johnson found that many rural youth remained surprisingly loyal to the traditional church—although he did note that those following this pattern were clustered around the ages of fourteen and fifteen and were at the "age that the most serious emotional shocks were observed in race attitudes and color consciousness." Other teen-age youth, on the other hand, were highly critical of emotional preachers and their sermons, were critical of the churches' double moral code, and turned elsewhere for the amusements such as dancing and movies that the church refused to countenance.[6] In analyzing the responses collected in twelve counties in the Black Belt, Johnson also detected some differences between the plantation and nonplantation areas. While the plantation areas remained ultra conservative, the nonplantation areas, which tended to be closer to urban areas and more influenced by them, were more susceptible to change. "The sermon is still directed to the older people, the church is still dominated by the deacons and other elders, emphasis is still on 'old-time religion,' and many forms of innocent recreation are still banned; occasionally, however, there is a disposition to provide within the church a substitute for worldly pleasures denied, and at the same time there is, as a result of an improved cultural level, a more serious emphasis upon a code of conduct consistent with the standards of the larger culture."[7] Johnson was hopeful that if the church would adapt itself to changing cultural patterns within the black community it could reassert its influence on black youth.[8]

When Harry V. Richardson undertook his study of the rural black church, he brought to it a heightened consciousness of the church as a potential agency of social and economic uplift. In his intensive survey of four counties scattered throughout the rural South, begun in 1944, Richardson was particularly interested in the quality of community and nonspiritual leadership which the church could give to the most impoverished and discriminated-against segment of American society, the Negro of the rural South. Some of the material found by Richardson updated findings reported by Mays and Nicholson and Johnson on the inferior training of the clergy, the prevalence of absentee pastors, the poverty of the members and the churches, and the inadequacy of programs of the church, especially for the young. But what disturbed Richardson even more was the failure of ministers to understand fully their parishoners' problems, to give any kind of meaningful cooperation to such trained leaders as county agents, home demonstration agents, or health officers. While the average sermon of the rural minister may have been less than stimulating, Richardson recognized that "the effective element in improving people is not preaching, but programs; not eloquence, but leadership in the activities of everyday life."[9] Rural ministers were all too inclined to class race relations as "good" if there had been no recent, overt violence. While acknowledging that militant protest on the part of a black minister could result in bloodshed, Richardson felt that more subtle avenues did exist by which a concerned and trained pastor could pursue his people's interest. In fact, for all the faith and loyalty of the laymen, the rural black church appeared to be little more than a fair-weather friend. Richardson made the startling discovery that in Northumberland County, Virginia, where the racial atmosphere was the least tense, expenditures for black education were highest, farm ownership among blacks equaled that among whites (73.6 percent), there were no superfluous churches, and membership reached a full 89.7 percent of the black population. In Mississippi County, Arkansas—where expenditures for black education were the lowest, where only 2.8 percent of the black farmers were full owners, where the racial atmosphere, while not as bad as in the two remaining counties, was nevertheless worse than in Northumberland—membership reached only 10 percent.[10] He concluded:

> When we turn to consider the work of the church in these social problems, a striking correlation at once comes to view: where living conditions are highest, church life is best; where living conditions are lowest, church life is poorest. . . . This makes inescapable the conclusion that in quality of service to its people, the rural church follows advantages (favored living conditions) instead of seeking to increase advantages for those who do not have them. It also means that quality of church life rises as living standards of the people rise. Therefore it is imperative that the church improve life among its people, for as the people improve, so does the church.[11]

Exhaustive as the above studies have been, this description of the rural church would not be complete without some reference to

Hylan Lewis's study of the small (population 4,000) southern Piedmont town he calls Kent. This study, carried out in the post-World War II years 1947 to 1949, suggests the quality of church life in the small rural town, in a transitional state between the tiny, isolated, open country church and the bewildering variety of the metropolitan religious scene. Three things stand out about black Protestantism in Kent. First is the high level of nominal church membership among the 1,000 black residents of Kent and the correspondingly low level of regular attendance. Lewis says that while over 90 percent of the population have belonged to a church at one time or another, "on any Sunday morning that is not a special occasion, only one-sixth of the total population and approximately one-third of the active church members will be found in church."[12] This situation, as has been noted elsewhere, may be described as the "state church effect," in which the church, "though it is an integrated part of the round of life and commands a high degree of nominal affiliation, . . . elicits the profound involvement of few."[13]

The second notable fact is that in a town with only three churches, differentiation of membership along class lines has appeared. While each area of concentration of the black population except one has a church, Lewis notes that "church attendance tends to follow preference lines rather than locality lines."[14] The Field's Street Methodist Episcopal Church has the smallest membership, smallest regular attendance, is the oldest and most restrained in its worship. The middle church, Mount Prospect African Methodist Episcopal Zion Church, is the largest and is more expressive than Field's Street. According to Lewis, "in the middle-class sense, this congregation tends to be progressive and aggressive and the church is one of their vehicles of expression." The Union Baptists do not have weekly services, have an absentee pastor, and in general have a more emotional, rural, "old-fashioned" approach to church services.[15]

The third noteworthy characteristic of the Kent churches is the range of outlets they offer their members for everything from traditional rituals to militant political involvement. On the traditional side, they continue to provide for the important ceremonies of life. Indeed, the stress Kent Protestants place on the church funeral reminds one of the emphasis this particular rite received in the slave church.[16] As Lewis notes, "an essential feature of religion and church membership is the expectation of a church funeral; indeed, it is one of the motives for maintaining church membership."[17] Much of the more formal socializing among the Kent Protestants is also connected to obligations incurred through membership in one of the auxiliary church organizations such as the Helpful Ladies Club or the Young Men's Betterment League. Yet the ill-defined goals of these groups tend to reduce their real worth for the church or community at large:

> The almost exclusive religious and church interest goes far to explain the relative stability of the Baptist men's group, in contrast to the other two men's groups. The other groups— although they operate under the aegis of the church and in their meetings and activities give symbolic and material support to the church—have ambitions for community-wide influence and a larger degree of independence from the church. The indecision that results from these conflicting purposes makes for ineffectiveness and lack of member interest. The women's clubs do not have the same problem because they are to a large extent controlled by social and status considerations.[18]

In Kent the two organizations concerned with racial betterment—the Fair Deal Democratic Club and the N.A.A.C.P.—had relatively small followings and seemed to be of less importance to the black community than church and fraternal groups. Yet, as Lewis observes, their true influence was difficult to measure and they represented potential power in times of crisis. The churches, especially those associated with black-controlled denominations, formed the organizational base, especially for the better-organized Fair Deal Democratic Club. "The significance of the church is seen in this organization by the following facts: the leaders and most active members of the group are either ministers or church officers; churches were used for purposes of circulating information and instructions; and the proceedings of the one business meeting held during the year the investigator was in the community were colored by the religious emphasis and ideology."[19]

The importance of the church to the spiritual, social, and interracial aspects of life in the black community of Kent seems indisputable. Yet this "state church" does not automatically lend its own prestige to occupants of its pulpits. The black minister of Kent is of far less importance than the prestige-laden undertaker:

> The functions of the [ministerial] office—preaching and presiding over significant ceremonies such as burial rites—are important; the individual minister is highly expendable locally and his prestige as a person may be low. . . . In actual practice, he has a rather tenuous hold on his job, and his leadership functions are made difficult by the limited expectations of the congregation, chronic financial problems, limitations related to training or personal characteristics, and a factionalism in the church that is inherent in the gap between young and old, traditionalists and progressives.[20]

### Urbanization and Differentiation

When Mays and Nicholson undertook their study of the Negro's church in 1930, they found it necessary to devote the bulk of their energies, and of the space in their report, to the phenomena of the black church in the city, especially the northern city. In little more than fifteen years, the social setting of black church life had undergone a tremendous transformation. As a result of massive migrations beginning in the second decade of the twentieth century, increasing numbers of black people found themselves forced to cope with life in the impersonal industrial centers of the North. The northern churches found themselves with overwhelming numbers of poor and often ignorant migrants whose spiritual and material needs frequently seemed beyond their capacity to serve. The story of the urban church in the postwar years is very largely an epic of established black Protestantism trying to meet a major crisis with limited material resources and, all too often, with limited imagination as well—and of a restless population first searching for renewal, at the old familiar altars, then turning to the storefronts, the Father Divines, the Black Muslims in their quest for a religion which could make the new and strange burdens of urban life somehow tolerable.

Referring to the *Federal Census of Religious Bodies* for 1916 and 1926 (surveys whose estimates both of membership and of number of churches they consider conservative), Mays and Nicholson note that for the five northern cities used in their analysis—Chicago, Detroit, Cincinnati, Philadelphia, and Baltimore—the census figures show a 151 percent increase in the number of black Baptist churches, and a 200 percent increase in Baptist membership between 1916 and 1926; the A.M.E. churches in these cities showed increases of 124 percent for number of churches, 85 percent for members.[21] Yet their own examination of 609 urban churches, North and South, suggested that the work of the church was generally carried on by less than half of the members, that many membership figures were inflated, and that in churches larger than 2,000 in membership (certainly an urban phenomenon) participation dwindles below the scant half shown by smaller congregations.[22] Mere expansion in numbers as reported in federal census data cannot be taken as certain testimony that the urban church was fulfilling its obligations.

Surveys of the services offered by the 609 churches in the study revealed the highly traditional character of their programs. All of the churches had preaching, union services and interchurch cooperation, missionary societies, and club work. More than 90 percent had Sunday school, poor relief, and revivals. Yet only 18 churches were involved in feeding the unemployed, 2 in running employment agencies, and 3 in sponsoring day nurseries.[23] At the heart of the problem, of course, lay the financial and leadership resources available to the besieged urban church. While the urban clergy compared favorably with the rural clergy with respect to training, fully three-quarters of the urban ministers had very limited training beyond high school.[24] Queries to the ministers and officers of the urban churches showed that 94.4 percent felt that their membership consisted predominantly of domestic workers and common laborers, with only 2.4 percent reporting a majority of members employed as skilled tradesmen, business, or professional people.[25] Although northern urban giving was slightly higher than southern urban giving, there was little money left for expanding the church program or the number of paid workers. Such money as did become available was quickly consumed by the "bare necessities" of salaries, interest and reduction of debt, repairs, and maintenance.[26] Of the 541 urban churches which owned or were purchasing their buildings at the time of the study, 386 were in debt. While many of the churches had acquired larger quarters to meet the challenge of the large number of migrants, the migrants did not carry their share of the increased financial responsibilities. The following comment and testimony indicate some of the difficulties inherent in ministering to the migrants:

It is the testimony of scores of ministers that the great increase in membership did not justify the increased financial outlay in church building. Many of the migrants were transitory—they came into the community as roomers and renters and moved frequently. Quite a number passed on to other cities after five or six months. Not a few lost church connections altogether in the northern community, which was so unlike the rural South from which many of them came. One pastor comments thus: "As a result of increased numbers owing to the migration, we had to find a new place. Our financial obligations were trebly increased; but really the financial help of migrants was not commensurate with their numbers. These people, many of them, came from the rural South with the habit of giving ten and twenty-five cents a month."[27]

Mays and Nicholson, while duly observing that there had been important psychological reasons for the proliferation of churches among blacks, finally concluded that the black people were over-churched in that what monies were available were spread too thinly among too many churches to be effective. Taking 500 as a minimum figure for effective size per church, they calculated that the number of excess churches ranged from 36 for Charleston and Philadelphia to 117 for Chicago and 124 for Birmingham.[28] Thus the northern urban church was clearly severely affected by the overchurching problem, even though it was approximately twice as wealthy as its southern counterpart. Mays and Nicholson were particularly critical of denominations, such as the Baptist, Holiness, and Spiritualist groups, that refused to supervise their own expansion, and of leaders reluctant to initiate consolidation among churches.[29]

*Impact of Proliferation and Differentiation on*
*the Northern Urban Church: Chicago*

It seems particularly fortunate that there should be a variety of solid studies on the church and its place in the black community for a key northern metropolis such as Chicago. The work of Vattel Daniel and of St. Clair Drake and Horace Cayton in the 1930s, and of Allan Spear, writing in the 1960s but dipping into the premigratory period of development, provide a composite picture of the changes during these crucial years in black church history.

Allan Spear notes that even before 1900, when integrated institutions were being sought, the church maintained a separatist stance. Between 1900 and 1915, however, when the old ideal was abandoned, various community institutions of their own were carved out by black leaders "that made the South Side not simply an area of Negro concentration but a city within a city."[30] Chicago's black churches doubled in number between 1900 and 1915, most being affiliated with the Baptist or the African Methodist Episcopal denominations. The larger, middle-class churches were expanding their activities into nonreligious spheres, but were already losing their appeal for some. Some of the upper classes were turning toward affiliations with the prestigious white denominations or to such experiments as Reverdy Ransom's Institutional Church. At the other end of the scale, the Holiness and Spiritualist churches were making their appearance on the religious scene:

> The Negro churches, then, were already self-sufficient by the end of the century and underwent no sudden or unprecedented changes between 1890 and 1915. But certain trends were apparent. The churches were broadening their programs to include a wide range of social activities. The large churches, dominated by the middle class, were still the most important religious institutions in the community, but they now faced competition from new churches, designed to meet the special needs of those at the upper and lower reaches of the social and economic spectrum. The migrations of the World War I period would rapidly accelerate these trends and profoundly change the religious life of the South Side.[31]

As might have been expected, the upper-class churches felt few reverberations from the migration, but the Holiness and Spiritualist churches mushroomed. In addition, newly formed Methodist and Baptist churches came to form a bridge between the "formal, old-time northern congregation and the emotional, uninhibited storefronts." Some older churches, such as Quinn Chapel (A.M.E.), gradually shifted status as a result of the new elements in church life, becoming known finally as "swank" churches. The one white denominational affiliate to feel the impact was St. Monica's Roman Catholic Church, which appealed to those who had been Catholic at home in Louisiana.[32]

Between 1937 and 1939 Vattel Daniel conducted an in-depth study of forty South Side churches and, on the basis of some 5,000 interviews, projected a class structure for the black community. In analyzing the churches he divided them into four different types: (1) the ecstatic cults or sects; (2) the semidemonstrative groups; (3) churches holding deliberative or sermon-centered services; and (4) the liturgical denominations.[33] While the traditional rural church closely approximated the urban designation of the semidemonstrative, the urban class structure no longer found this single type of service sufficient for its tastes. Daniel suggests that much of the evolution of the higher status churches had occurred by the time the first wave of migrants arrived, forcing the migrants to create services more in their own image. Dividing the black population into upper, upper-middle, lower-middle, and lower classes on the basis of "occupation, income, consumption, education, philosophy of life, pattern of behavior, associational activity, and family life," he suggests that the four types of churches reflect the degree of adjustment achieved by each class of a minority race.[34] Daniel concludes:

> The social nature of the bizarre behavior of the ecstatic sects prevents that type of isolation that accentuates inferiority and takes the devotee into a world where temporarily he can live above the handicaps of everyday life. The congenial informality of the semidemonstrative church group affords fellowship, personal recognition, and tension release, so consoling to the former ruralite in the urban situation. The members of the deliberative and of the liturgical churches seem already to have adjusted themselves to city life and their church services stress meeting squarely on the issues of life rather than seeking escape through emotional release.[35]

St. Clair Drake and Horace Cayton's study of Chicago's South Side, also conducted during the late 1930s, rounds out the class dimensions of urban black religiosity suggested by Daniel, and so enlarges upon the role the church has come to occupy since the migration north began. Drake and Cayton seem in nearly perfect agreement with Daniel that "the function of the church in orienting the upper class toward its world is extremely limited."[36] In discussing the middle class, these researchers have tended to emphasize popular concern for "saving the youth," expectations that preachers be staunch "race men," and a tendency to belong to large "mixed" churches which include some lower class elements. Daniel, Drake, and Cayton also paint essentially the same portrait of lower class religion, with its tension between the devout (a majority of them women) and disdainful sinners on the outside.[37]

Drake and Cayton have gone beyond Daniel, however, in trying to assess the real power and influence of the church in Chicago. Perhaps one of the most surprising findings in light of the general stereotype of the otherworldliness of black religion is Bronzeville's expectation that the church be a race institution.[38] Even in this metropolitan setting, where there are fully developed upper and upper-middle classes, only 10 percent of churches and less than 10 percent of attenders are affiliated with predominantly white denominations.[39] And in spite of the fact that most churches place greatest emphasis on their Sunday worship services (note Mays and Nicholson's figures cited earlier), Drake and Cayton posit that the greatest outreach lies elsewhere. "The largest proportion of people who maintain relationships with the church probably do so, except in very small congregations, through sub-organizations. In fact, many persons have their only relationship in this indirect manner. Such associated organizations range from purely social clubs to co-operative stores. Yet were it not for the primacy of the worship service, and for the hard labor of the sustaining members (predominantly women), the average church could not maintain itself."[40]

While the church, according to Drake and Cayton, no longer occupies the central position in the community which it did before the migration, it remains an important facet of urban life and a popular topic of conversation. The church's comparative wealth and the harsh conditions precipitated by the Depression in the black community seem to have unleashed many resentments against the church—some based on realism, others on an undue, if understandable, skepticism about the community's "oldest and wealthiest institution." The most prevalent indictments were: "(1) Church is a 'racket,' (2) Too many churches, (3) Churches are too emotional, (4) There's no real religion among the members, (5) Churches are a waste of time and money, (6) Ministers don't practice what they preach, (7) Ministers don't preach against 'sin,' (8) Church places too much emphasis upon money, (9) Negroes are too religious."[41]

These authors also noted with interest that when the staunchest supporters of the church defended their cherished institution against the naysayers within and without the church, many pointed to what services the church had done for "the race." The role of the preacher in such an atmosphere becomes doubly precarious. For while a preacher is supposed to support the race, whenever he promotes black businesses or others which hire blacks or tries to throw support behind a particular political candidate, he opens himself to the charge of "racketeering."[42]

### Storefront and Cult

Much of the preceding discussion has been devoted to the strains sustained by the urban church during a period of stressful change. Many churches established special programs and greatly expanded their memberships and physical plants in an effort to minister to the new arrivals. But one of the most visible accompaniments of the migration was the appearance of large numbers of storefront or house churches. Allan Spear has noted the presence of Spiritualist and Holiness churches in Chicago prior to World War I, but only with the coming of the southern migrants did they become a booming segment of the religious life of the city. Mays and Nicholson, too, noted the virtually uncontrolled proliferation of storefronts of the Spiritualist, Holiness, and even Baptist persuasions, and admitted that this uncontrolled growth was a key factor in the overchurching and sometimes poor churching of the cities. Mays and Nicholson also attempted, if briefly, to suggest some reason for the phenomenon. In spite of the fact that many rural people could find a comfortable niche in the larger churches, others who had enjoyed leadership positions in the rural South saw themselves relegated to the sidelines in the big urban churches. Some also found the sophistication of these churches too inhibiting. Frustrated leaders apparently encountered little difficulty in gathering together other migrants who missed the more intimate, freer services which they had enjoyed in their rural churches back home.[43] Drake and Cayton noted that the ritual the migrants were accustomed to could be found in several of the large churches which had made special efforts to oblige the migrants: "Probably the really important factor is the desire to belong to a small face-to-face group, to 'know everybody.' "[44]

Although Ira Harrison's study of the storefronts was carried out in the early 1960s, his insights seem applicable to the urban situation throughout the post-migration period. He quite rightly cautions against viewing the storefront as a means of "adaptation" for the rural migrant, for the storefront did not necessarily support those values, such as education, which are generally considered crucial to success in the larger society. Harrison noted how frequently the storefront members seemed to know each other and even to have come from the same locale in the South, thus presumably having many common associations in the past to add meaning to their present arrangement.[45] Harrison views these churches as fitting Anthony F. C. Wallace's model of a revitalization movement.[46] "They are deliberate, conscious, organized efforts of migrants to create a more satisfying mode of existing by refurbishing rural religious behavior to an urban environment."[47] Those who turned to the storefronts cannot really be viewed, then, as men and women who have lost their bearings in a new and frightening situation; rather, they are individuals who recognize the disorganizing influences of the city in one way or another and have sought to secure their moorings.[48]

Others, for varying reasons, found that even the fundamentalist, ecstatic Protestantism of the storefront and house churches was insufficient to their social, psychological, and religious requirements. Arthur Fauset, who made the initial attempt to examine the urban cults as a group, has suggested that they may well "be a continuation of the very kind of adaptation of an institution to a given need against which the slaveholders hope to safeguard themselves by forbidding Negroes to congregate even for purposes of religious worship."[49] The institution Fauset is referring to here is the Americar black church and the need he mentions is for a sense of national identity. Fauset views the "political" aspects of such groups as the black Jews and the Moorish Americans as one manifestation of a new determination on the part of a broad spectrum of Americans that America belongs to them, a feeling stimulating activism in trade unions, economic boycotts, and so on, among those who are not attracted to the type of nationalism offered by the cults.[50] However much the specific tenets of some of the cults may vary, it does seem that for most, the strengthening of self-esteem among members of a minority group is a major function.

Father Divine, who required the sacrifice of material wealth and worldly ties for entrance into his kingdoms, offered more than faith healing and a bounteous table. Father Divine was, according to two students of the movement, "sincere and aggressive in his fight for Negro equality." He opposed every aspect of segregation and conspicuously refrained from using terms denoting color in his publications, also prohibiting their use among the "reborn" children.[51]

The black Jews, on the other hand, seem to combine the familiar forms of southern religion with certain esteem-giving beliefs and practices. As Howard Brotz observes: "The ritual, the worship service, and even their basic theological conceptions have never departed very far from that which was familiar to these people in their childhood religious experience." They exhibited what Brotz calls the characteristics of the "pariah religiosity of the lower-class Negro church, organized around self-appointed, untrained, and uneducated preachers with a 'call,' in groups which have considerable flexibility in practice."[52] Yet the black Jews, under the leadership of a dark skinned charismatic leader such as the largely self-educated Rabbi Matthew, an emigrant from the West Indies, have claimed an honored and ancient ancestry and a religion which antedates that of the oppressive white majority. The group actively pursues such "non-Negro" habits as industry and restraint and avoids the use of pork. In spite of the fact that most whites (with the exception of some curious Jews) and the old and new Negro elites regarded the black Jews as merely another lower-class cult, Brotz suggests there is some evidence that "the self-esteem which individuals derive from membership in all these nationalistic sects has resulted in modification of behavior in the direction of personal stability."[53]

The Black Muslims seem to represent the ultimate development of the nationalistic cults with religious base. Not only have they departed most extremely in ritual from other lower-class Protestant groups, but they have not contented themselves with providing self-esteem for an outcast race. Their aim has been militant protest accompanied by an almost unprecedented rejection of the American value system. While rejecting white men as devils, and having a corresponding disregard for Christianity, they have gone a step beyond the fanaticism of white supremacist groups or the mainstream protest of other black groups by totally rejecting even the principles of the American creed, an extravagance which C. Eric Lincoln suggests may have put the Muslims beyond the pale of general acceptability by the black community.[54] Yet testimonies of early converts who came under the influence of the Prophet Farad Muhammad between 1930 and 1934 in the ghettos of Detroit reveal that for some, life in the northern city had made eminently acceptable a cult which condoned hatred of whites and told blacks of their right to exact an eye-for-an-eye justice.[55]

*Overviews of the Black Church*

Out of the multitudes of interviews and statistics on the black church gathered by scores of researchers during this era of upheaval and of increased awareness of the significance of the black church, three views of the church remain as a kind of intellectual dowry for the churchmen and researchers of the 1960s and 1970s. It is impossible to enter upon any prolonged discussion of the church without eventually referring to the ideas of Benjamin Mays and Joseph Nicholson, the synthesis of Gunnar Myrdal, and the hovering cynicism of E. Franklin Frazier.

Mays and Nicholson agreed that the image of the church which their research findings displayed was not very heartening. Pedestrian programs, inadequately trained leaders, overchurching, poor financial bases, and mounting debts were found in too many cases for them to give the black church an entirely clean bill of health. They realized, however, that what the black church was could not be entirely captured in columns of black and red: "The authors believe that there is in the genius or the 'soul' of the Negro church something that gives it life and vitality, that makes it stand out significantly above its buildings, creeds, rituals, and doctrines, something which makes it a unique institution."[56] For one thing, "The Negro church is the most thoroughly owned and controlled public institution of the race," and while total indebtedness figures might seem threatening, most churches owed relatively little, were largely self-sustaining, and anyway were of little use to creditors for repossession purposes. Further, "The opportunity found in the Negro church to be recognized, and to be 'somebody,' has stimulated the pride and preserved the self-respect of many Negroes who would have been entirely beaten by life, and possibly completely submerged." While admitting that this rather democratic practice may account for much of the untrained leadership which continues to plague the church, Mays and Nicholson refuse to underrate the psychological importance this has had for the black community. Mays and Nicholson also refuse to denigrate the function of the church as a place to relax, whether this freedom from restraint manifests itself in the violent emotionalism of some of the storefront groups or simply in "a nodding of the head as the minister preaches." It is the one place where black people can be themselves, without fear, and what is made of this time may well be up to the minister.[57]

Mays and Nicholson also saw the church as community center, supporter of education and black business, and still essentially classless. But perhaps above all was the freedom and social action potential of the black ministry, for "all things considered, it is easier for the man who is down to see wrongs and injustices and in many cases easier for him to become an apostle of righteousness." Given the poverty and commitment of the laymen, Mays and Nicholson believed that with the right leadership "the Negro church has the potentialities to become possibly the greatest spiritual force in the United States."[58] Perhaps not until the late 1960s would so strong a belief in this singular black institution again be voiced.

As a white man and a foreigner, Gunnar Myrdal may have been forced to rely a little more heavily on hard statistics to interpret this prominent institution of a circumscribed race. Yet because he lacked much of the personal commitment of Mays and Nicholson, the fact that he reached a similar recognition of the intangible value of the black church is impressive. He found that among both blacks and whites, competition among a host of churches for loyal members had resulted in "a fundamental democratization of organized religious life in America."⁵⁹ Yet unlike Mays and Nicholson, Myrdal detected a highly stratified church life among blacks, in which membership in various denominations denoted specific class levels. Myrdal concludes that "viewed as an instrument of collective action to improve the Negroes' position in American society, the church has been relaticely inefficient and uninfluential." Yet he puts this in the context of the behavior of Christian churches in general which "have, for the most part, conformed to the power situation of the time and locality." Still, the otherworldliness and tendency to avoid real issues are there, and the schismatic tendencies of Negro churches, the well-known plague of overchurching, weaken the church further; Myrdal also suggests that poverty may make the church somewhat dependent on funds from whites, and quite realistically observes that the typically low salaries which most black churches can scrape together are ill-suited to attracting the kind of quality leadership envisioned by Mays and Nicholson. In fact, at that moment black preachers appeared to be lagging, not leading.⁶⁰ Yet at this point Myrdal arrives at the attribute of the church which seems to set it apart, which may or may not be a separate "genius," but at least represents some form of fusion with the soul and personality of its people:

When discussing the Negro church as it is and as it might come to be, it must never be forgotten that *the Negro church fundamentally is an expression of the Negro community itself.* If the church has been otherworldly in outlook and indulged in emotional ecstasy, it is primarily because the downtrodden common Negroes have craved religious escape from poverty and other tribulations. . . .

When the Negro community changes, the church also will change. . . . That this fundamental truth is understood—underneath all bitter criticism—is seen in the fact that Negro intellectuals are much more willing to cooperate with Negro churches than white intellectuals with white churches. The Negro protest and improvement organizations cooperate with all "respectable" Negro churches. The solidarity behind the abstract church institution in the Negro community is simply amazing. The visitor finds everywhere a widespread criticism, but this is focused mainly on the preachers. Few question the church as such, its benevolent influence and its great potentialities.[61]

E. Franklin Frazier, who for many years occupied a position as an unquestioned leader of American sociologists, has written a brief polemic on the black church which in many scholarly circles has passed for the last word on the subject. In the sections of the book in which he utilizes the researches of Mays and Nicholson, Drake and Cayton, Daniel, Fauset, and others, his conclusions vary little from theirs. He too agrees that the church became secularized in the urban environment, concerning itself more with the worldly well-being of its members and supporting such "practical" organizations as the N.A.A.C.P. and the Urban League. But the crucial problem of overchurching is dismissed as "irrelevant in a sense when one considers the important role of the Negro church in the organization of the Negro community."[62] Likewise, when he considers the question of assimilation, which he assumes to be continuing apace, we find that with the church, "the most important cultural institution created by Negroes, one encounters the most important institutional barrier to integration and the assimilation of Negroes."[63] Further, the church has lost much of its influence and can no longer serve as a "refuge" from whites. He accepts Vattel Daniel's description of the upper class as finding the church relatively unimportant. His middle class, unlike Daniel's, however, seems to attend churches primarily for reasons of nostalgia, status, or business. Most interesting perhaps is his depiction of gospel singers as "an accommodation between traditional Negro religion and the new outlook of Negroes in the new American environment"—and as the form of religious life now favored among the lower classes.[64] We find, in fact, that the institution which has so frequently been characterized as giving people with little status in the outer world a chance to participate and build feelings of self-worth is indeed an "authoritarian" institution. The authoritarian pattern set by the church has been repeated in other black organizations, leaving blacks with "little education in democratic processes." Further, the institution which has enduringly supported educational institutions of varying caliber is summarily dismissed as anti-intellectual:

The Negro church and Negro religion have cast a shadow over the entire intellectual life of Negroes and have been responsible for the so-called backwardness of American Negroes. . . . It is only as a few Negro individuals have been able to escape from the stifling domination of the church that they have been able to develop intellectually and in the field of art. This development is only being achieved on a broader scale to the extent that Negroes are being integrated into the institutions of the American community and as the social organization of the Negro community, in which the church is the dominant element, crumbles as the 'walls of segregation come tumbling down.'[65]

With Frazier's writings the overviews of the church had covered a full 180 degrees. Whether Frazier's view of the church would reign supreme, or whether thought on the subject would come full circle would greatly depend on what developed on the assimilationist front in the 1960s.

As noted in the first chapter, the primary purpose of this study is the assessment of whether black religiosity is basically otherworldly and an opiate of civil rights militancy or is temporal and an inspiration of militancy. From analyses of spirituals and the religion of slaves the dual nature of religion—as inspiration and opiate—can be noted. With emancipation and then with Reconstruction, the black church and black religion continued to have this dual nature. On the one hand, religion held by blacks who resided in rural areas and in the South and who had lower levels of education appeared to be otherworldly; at least the stereotype of blacks as having a passive orientation to temporal problems, coupled with an emotional "pie in the sky by and by" religious outlook, would give us this impression. On the other hand, the black church provided considerable organization for the black community, building solidarity or cohesion and supporting to the extent possible civil rights activism. The black church also supported the educational advances of black Americans. Various studies have been reviewed which would support the thesis that the black church did in fact provide organization for the community, both rural and urban, and at least rudimentary support for civil rights militancy. At the same time, that the church had faults and faced considerable difficulty in adjusting to the fact that many of its members were poorly educated and were migrants has not been glossed over in this institutional analysis of the black church.

With the migration of blacks to the North and to cities, especially in the World War I period, a considerable degree of acculturation began occurring on the part of blacks vis-à-vis the middle-class culture of the urban society.[66] Not only did blacks have more access to the urban culture, but the city provided considerable freedom for the further development of black institutions, including the church. Relocation also meant rising educational levels and an expansion of job opportunities.

By the late 1950s and early 1960s the black community was especially anxious that a formal change occur in regard to the status of the black man in America; such a change would involve the lowering of race barriers, the passage of civil rights bills, and a greater movement toward an integrated society. This feeling of readiness was not new, however. A spirit of militancy had long been present in the black community, nurtured by black institutions and especially by the black church which had reminded its followers that they were God's people and that justice would eventually come to exist on earth.

The civil rights movement had tremendous implications for the black ministry, the black church, and black religion, for no longer would the church have to overemphasize the passive side of religion. In the late 1930s it was noted that, increasingly, black ministers in urban areas were expected to be race men. By the civil rights period even the rural churches and ministers were expected to support workers for the civil rights movement publicly, and, indeed, many of these churches became centers for such activities.

# 4:

## Racial Differences in
## Religious Dimensions

Our next task is to examine racial differences in various dimensions of religiosity and in receptivity toward the church's involvement in civil rights protest. The stereotype would say that blacks are more emotional in their religion and thus more otherworldly than this-worldly. Consequently, religion would serve as an opiate for civil rights activism. Such a view can be dispelled by showing that blacks are not more likely than whites to report having had religious experiences, that blacks do not turn with greater frequency to prayer, and that blacks are not more likely to subscribe to a conservative religious ideology. On the other hand, if the black church is of special importance to the black community for the purpose of solidarity or organization, then we would expect blacks to attend church more often than whites. Furthermore, we might expect that as blacks increasingly believed that integration was occurring, their greater church attendance (relative to that of white Protestants) would fall off. This trend analysis will be presented in the concluding chapter.

Besides examining racial differences in these various dimensions of religiosity, we will explore more directly what individuals want in their ministers and churches; for example, were there racial differences in attitudes toward the march on Washington (which was to include a number of ministers), toward having their ministers involved in civil rights protesting, and toward Martin Luther King, Jr.? If stereotype would picture blacks more otherworldly in religion, then concomitantly, blacks would not be particularly militant about temporal, racial concerns. We will see that a considerable attitudinal difference existed between the races in regard to receptivity to civil rights, with blacks being much more likely to favor civil rights protest, even though such activities often included their ministers. Blacks desire a more active role on the part of their churches, believing they should take a positive stand on social and political questions, as we will see from a trends analysis of data on this subject.

Parenthetically, it should be noted that all Gallup data available on these subjects from the late 1950s through the 1960s were analyzed. Generally one set of data per religious dimension was available, although, luckily, two sets were available for the ideological dimension. Some nineteen separate surveys were available for the trends analysis on church attendance. All surveys conducted by the Gallup organization during this period which included items useful for assessing the dimensions of religion or receptivity to civil rights protest on the part of ministers or churches were included for secondary analysis in this study. Of course it cannot be said that no pertinent surveys were inadvertently omitted. A thorough search was made of survey question files maintained by the Roper Public Opinion Research Center, Williams College (the copy of the file used is located at Western Kentucky University). Finally, several additional sets of data were used at appropriate places in the study when Gallup data were not available. The samples will be described as the studies are introduced.

The basic data handling technique employed in this study is Multiple Classification Analysis which permits the examination of the interrelationships among several predictor variables and a dependent variable.[1] In the computer runs, two sets of predictor variables were generally employed: (a) race, education, region, and residence, and (b) sex, age, race, education, occupation, region, and residence. When racial differences were being explored, the context for such analysis was that various background characteristics, being linked with acculturation, might be operative in influence, and here the first set of predictor variables was deemed important. Various studies have shown that education, region, and residence are linked with both religious and civil rights orientations. For example, individuals with lower levels of education, from the South, and from rural areas of residence are more likely to be fundamentalist in religious ideology. On the other hand, acculturation into the urban culture of America would mean the gradual disappearance of such a religious orientation on the part of the group undergoing such acculturation. Education has been coded from low to high (the categories are given later in this chapter), while region has been categorized as South and non-South and residence as nonmetropolitan and metropolitan. These variables, then, are interpreted as ordered rather than being at the nominal level of measurement. Because the Gallup organization earlier used nonwhite-white as racial identification and later switched to black-white-other nonwhite, race here has been coded as nonwhite-white or black-white (when using the latter identification, other nonwhites are deleted in the analysis). From visual examination of means produced by the MCA printout, the direction of the effect of each predictor is indicated by the adding of signs.

Our attention will be on racial differences. Where the dependent variable is a dimension of religiosity, the analysis is limited to Protestants only, since the great majority of blacks are Protestants, while a sizable proportion of whites are Catholics for whom the dimensions under study make less sense (for example, the ideological dimension as operationalized has less validity for Catholics). Black culture has been largely influenced by the predominantly Protestant preference of black Americans. Besides examining racial differences, it was desired to examine separately the effects of the various predictors on the dependent variable for blacks only. Our attention here will not be on whites, but rather on blacks. For these reasons, together with limitations of computer time, separate tables were not run for whites-only, white Protestants only, or black Protestants only, except in several rare instances.

The second set of variables includes, in addition to those variables indicated in the first set, sex, age, and occupation. These variables have been shown to be related both to civil rights orientation and to religiosity. When racial differences are examined for attitudes toward protest, these additional variables are utilized.

Finally it might be asked how each predictor variable might be related to such dimensions of religiosity as prayer and attendance. That is, what are the theoretical reasons for including such variables as sex (coded female-male), age (34 and under, 35-44, 45-54, and 55 and over), education (8th grade or less, 9th-11th grades, high school completed, and some college or more), occupation (blue-collar versus white-collar), region, and residence? Too often these variables have been used, together with other variables such as stage of the family life cycle and number of generations of American citizenship, with little theoretical explanation. For example, it has been reported by several researchers that females show more interest in religion than males, perhaps because of different socialization of males and females in regard to their social roles. The relationship between age and church attendance, as one dimension of religiosity, is less clear, but the traditional view is that church attendance shows an increase by people entering their mid-thirties (it was also higher for adolescents) and decreases in old age. High levels of church attendance and religious fervor are usually associated with the southern region of the United States, since it is that region where fundamentalism is more frequently found. This culture pattern can probably be traced to the revivals of the early 1800s which occurred in the border-South and South. In general white-collar workers are more likely to attend church than blue-collar workers. Similarly, education and church attendance are positively related. Traditionally, church attendance is seen as slightly diminishing in the city; and religious conservatism is viewed as being more prevalent in rural areas. These are, however, empirical finds and based on little theory.

It might be suggested that individuals have perceptions of responsibility which motivate them and influence their public religious life. Such a view assumes that individuals value positive evaluations by others (for example, being accorded high status), and that at a less conscious level their behaviors reflect prior socialization. The desire for positive evaluation would be coupled with their fulfilling role expectations. American society has embraced public religion warmly in comparison to, let us say, countries of Western Europe. To be American is to be religious, to have a religious preference, to attend church, and to give lip service, at least, to the importance of being religious.[2] Therefore religious behavior and the holding of certain beliefs would be expected on the part of individuals who were attempting to fulfill certain roles and who desired positive evaluation. Further, some individuals because of their status and role are more open to public criticism or at least come to feel some burden of responsibility to do what is expected of them (as they perceive the American value system). For example, women are expected to be the prime socializers of their children and as part of this to teach their offspring morals. This they accomplish in part by being examples themselves, attending church and evincing religious interests. Men are assigned roles that are more instrumental than social-emotional and thus are less concerned with problems of morality and socialization. Consequently, men are less likely to attend worship services. Some individuals feel more protected from public censure or do not feel affected by it; here the findings that certain professionals such as doctors, lawyers, and college professors are less likely to attend church might be explained by noting that these professionals have technical occupational skills which the community generally respects and needs, and, furthermore, their professional ideologies include compartmentalizing public opinion and community pressures. Age can also be analyzed from this viewpoint; young people are quite subject to their parents' commands and partly as a response to this there is high attendance for early adolescents. Later, on the other hand, attendance decreases until they reach their early thirties, when they become committed to the materialistic goals of the society—making house payments, car payments, and attempting job advancement. For these individuals, especially in smaller communities where public opinion is generally more effective, increased church attendance would be likely as they become more liable to community pressure. It is likely that more traditional religious behaviors and attitudes would be found in rural areas, since rural people presumably would feel more a part of a gemeinschaft society, having more primary ties and being better known among a circle of friends. In general, individuals of a higher social class are more liable to such pressures since, presumably, they are more involved in materialistic strivings; yet class and religious activity are not related in a linear fashion, since upper-class individuals are freed from being oriented to conformist pressures from the general society. Most open to such pressures would probably be members of the lower-middle class and members of certain professions. Education, as a variable which partly determines social class, would be positively related to religious activity of a public nature.

Southerners would also be generally more likely to participate in public religion than northerners since the culture pattern emphasizes religion and since smaller communities predominate in the South. One would speculate that southern women, especially, would exhibit a high level of public religion.

In a comparison of the religiosity of blacks and whites, acculturation is a pertinent concept. Past differences in religiosity, (for example, blacks being more conservative in their religious ideology than whites) might well have been linked with black-white differentials in regard to residential and regional locations and educational levels. In addition, lag in acculturation can occur, with first-generation city dwellers, for example, being more conservative in ideology than third-generation urban residents. Should a significant relationship between one of the acculturation factors (for example, education) and a dimension of religiosity (such as reporting a religious experience) be found for blacks but not for whites, a direct comparison of blacks and whites on the dimension of religiosity under examination will not be especially meaningful since interaction is present and since Multiple Classification Analysis assumes an additive model. Such an interaction might be interpreted as lag in acculturation, with possibly the dimension having lost saliency for whites. This explanation will be spelled out in greater detail later in the chapter.

The direction of empirical research in the sociology of religion was established by Gerhard Lenski, who suggested that religiosity is multidimensional. Lenski's four variables were developed in order to indicate causal relationships, for example, "devotionalism . . . seems linked both with the spirit of capitalism and with a humanitarian outlook when confronted with problems of social injustice."[3] Of course Lenski is especially addressing himself to white religion since the bulk of his Detroit sample was white.

A parallel development of variables was begun by Glock and his students. Stark and Glock, however, explicitly separated the "motives for commitment and the consequences which follow from it"; and, consequently, Glock's five (especially the first four) dimensions were at the descriptive level, which, it might be noted, is more easily investigated by survey research methods.[4]

To the question of whether "religious commitment is empirically a unitary or multidimensional phenomenon," Stark and Glock reply that the dimensions of religiosity which they have developed "are much more independent of one another than they are measures of the same thing."[5] After analyzing data from 362 college students, Faulkner and De Jong concluded that the "diversity in the degree of relationships [among the five dimensions of religiosity] lends empirical support to the view that religious involvement is characterized by several dimensions—some of which are more closely related than others."[6] Finally, Lenski, as noted, conceived of religiosity as multidimensional.[7] This attempt to break out the dimensions as more separate than part and parcel of one another has come under recent criticism. Clayton, also using student data, observed substantial positive associations among four dimensions of religiosity (ritualistic, experiential, ideological, and intellectual) and moderate positive associations between each of these four dimensions and the consequential dimension. He suggests that these dimensions (as measured by Faulkner and De Jong) "are perhaps not as 'independent' as they sometimes appear."[8] In conclusion, the dimensions as outlined by Glock and his students may be more unitary than was first believed. Rather than settling this issue, investigators are now going beyond the question to a newer topic, salience of religion.[9] In this study the various dimensions will generally be considered separately, since the dimensions may relate in different directions with a given dependent variable, such as civil rights militancy.

The salience of religion, that is, the importance of religion or the interest the individual has in religion, is in many respects an old friend, since it is what Lenski was trying to measure: the "religious factor," or the impact of religious forces upon individual attitudes and behaviors. Here Lenski especially focused upon the role of devotionalism in contrast to that of doctrinal orthodoxy which appeared to be linked with a "compartmentalized view of life" that seemed to "foster the view that one's religious commitments are irrelevant to one's political and economic actions and other aspects of secular life."[10] Lenski was also interested in the type of involvement the individual had with the socioreligious group, and here he developed two measures, communalism and associational involvement. The former was linked with "fostering intergroup tension and hostility," while the latter meant the reverse, or as Lenski writes, "in the case of Protestants, both Negro and white, those who were more active in the churches were a bit *more* likely to express favorable views of other groups than those who were less involved.[11] The topic of religious saliency will be considered later in this study.

*Dimensions of Religiosity Utilized*
*for Data Analysis*

This chapter is concerned with racial comparisons on the different dimensions of religiosity. In the secondary analysis of Gallup data to be reported here, the multidimensional taxonomy proposed by Glock and Stark was adopted with modification. Included are the experiential (experiencing), ideological (holding to certain beliefs), ritualistic (praying, worshiping, and the like), intellectual (being informed about the faith), and consequential dimensions.[12] Stark and Glock note that the last dimension, encompassing the secular effects of the other dimensions of religiosity on the individual, differs from the other dimensions in being perhaps more dependent than independent.[13] Yinger has commented that "it is perhaps unfortunate that they reduce the clarity of their list by putting what is primarily a dependent variable into a list of independent or intervening variables."[14] In this secondary analysis the consequential dimension has been excluded.

Lenski, with his earlier multidimensional conceptualization of religious commitment, investigated two religious orientations— doctrinal orthodoxy ("assent to prescribed doctrines") and devotionalism ("that orientation which emphasizes the importance of private, or personal, communion with God").[15] As noted elsewhere, "The doctrinal orthodoxy orientation seems to be equivalent to Glock and Stark's ideological dimension; but the devotionalism orientation is not compatible with Glock and Stark's ritualistic dimension, for Lenski . . . also conceived of group involvement, consisting of the individual's being involved in either the association (the church, as measured by attendance, for example) or the sub-community (limiting primary relations to one's own socioreligious group)."[16] Consequently, the ritualistic dimension in Glock and

Stark's taxonomy would include both Lenski's devotionalism measure and associational involvement. Therefore, the ritualistic dimension has been separated into prayer and attendance in this secondary analysis.[17]

### The Experiential Dimension

This chapter is concerned with racial differences in the various dimensions of religiosity as just discussed. Stereotype would have blacks more "religious," a term which would include being more emotional (or more likely to report having had a religious experience) than whites. Glock and Stark have provided an extended elaboration of this experiential dimension.[18] Here the dimension will be examined in a fairly cursory fashion; that is, it will simply be determined whether racial differences exist for the basic dimension. The data come from a February 1962 Gallup survey. The interviewees were asked: "Would you say that you have ever had a religious or mystical experience—that is, a moment of sudden religious insight or awakening?"

The statement by E. T. Krueger that "religion is to the Negro what music and poetry are to the white man" clearly shows the influence of the stereotype of the religious black man. "If the stereotype were based in fact," as is pointed out in *The Black Church in America,* "we should be able to assume that Negroes would be more likely to report having had a religious experience."[19] Knowing that blacks have undergone the great migration to the North and to the cities, we should expect no black-white differences in the reporting of such experiences, since scoring high on this variable would be more characteristic of southerners (on this point the reader can turn to the volume by Hill describing southern religion).[20] An examination of overall percentages by race led to an earlier conclusion that there were no racial differences on this variable,[21] but here a closer examination will be made using Multiple Classification Analysis, a technique that, in simplest terms, permits entering a number of factors into the analysis, with each factor acting as a control on every other factor used to describe (or predict) the dependent variable, which in this case is reporting not having had or reporting having had such an experience. The influ-

*Table 1*

Effects of Race, Education, Region, and Residence
on the Experiential Dimension of Religiosity
(February 1962 Data, Protestants Only)

| Predictors | Eta Coefficient | Beta Coefficient |
|---|---|---|
| Race | +.00[a] | +.02[a] |
| Education | -.05[a] | -.04[a] |
| Region | -.17 | -.17 |
| Residence | -.03[a] | -.00[a] |

NOTE: N=1,903, R=.171 (d.f.=7) (used up).
[a]Not significant at the .05 level, using appropriate F test of significance. Unless indicated, all other coefficients are significant at the .01 level.

ence of each of the factors entered into the analysis can be determined both without and with the presence of the other explanatory factors. The degree of relationship between the factor, such as race, and the phenomenon under study, is indicated by the eta coefficient (without the presence of other explanatory factors) and by the beta coefficient (with the presence of other explanatory factors). Table 1 includes a summary of the effects of race, education, region, and residence for all Protestants. Education was categorized as: 8th grade or less, 9th through 11th grades, high school diploma, and some college or more. Region was dichotomized into South and non-South.[22] Residence was dichotomized as nonmetropolitan (less than 50,000 population) and metropolitan. Of the 263 black Protestants (here other nonwhites were excluded in the analysis), 24.3 percent reported such an experience (adjusting for the effects of the other predictors gives 22.3 percent), compared to 24.8 percent of the whites (25.1 percent, adjusted). As expected, region was an especially important predictor. On the other hand, residential differences were not found.[23] Of the 737 southerners, 34.2 percent (both unadjusted and adjusted for the effects of the other predictors) reported affirmatively compared to 18.7 percent (unadjusted and adjusted) of the nonsoutherners.

If the stereotype of the black American as being emotional in

*Table 2*

Effects of Education, Region, and Residence
on the Experiential Dimension of Religiosity
(February 1962 Data, Blacks Only)

| Predictors | Eta Coefficient | Beta Coefficient |
|---|---|---|
| Education | -.23 | -.22 |
| Region | -.21 | -.19 |
| Residence | -.11[b] | -.03[a] |

NOTE: N=299, R=.274 (d.f.=6).
[a]Not significant at the .05 level, using appropriate F test of significance.
Unless indicated, all other coefficients are significant at the .01 level.
[b]Significant at the .05 level.

religion had any truth in the past, we might expect to find traces among the less educated, the rural, and the southern, since presumably these individuals would be less likely to have incorporated the urban, middle-class culture which would de-emphasize emotional religious experience. In Table 2 the coefficients are shown for blacks only. Here non-Protestant blacks are not excluded in the analysis. Both education and region were inversely related to experiential religiosity as indicated by the reporting of having had a mystical religious experience. Residence, inversely related without the effects of the other two variables held constant, was not significantly related with the effects of education and region controlled.

In comparing the coefficients presented in Tables 1 and 2, it can be seen that education is inversely related to experiential religiosity for blacks but is unrelated to this dimension for the entire sample. Consequently, possible interaction effects must be noted, namely, that the effect of education may be different when race is specified. The data were rerun for white Protestants only and the resulting coefficients were almost identical, with no significant relationship between education and experiential religiosity.

In sum, for both whites and blacks region is inversely related to experiential religiosity, with southerners more likely to report a religious experience; this finding substantiates Hill's claim that southern religion insists on directly experiencing God.[24] It is speculated that experiential religiosity was once inversely correlated with social class (which includes education) but is now simply a part of southern culture. Southern religious bodies insisting on direct experience, while once sectarian, today more often than not are middle class in terms of membership; and consequently the requirement of a direct religious experience for entrance into membership has been routinized and, in effect, gutted of lasting meaning to most participants. In regard to the experiential dimension of religiosity, blacks probably lag behind whites in acculturation to urban, middle-class culture which would include bland religious forms; thus for blacks education and experiential religiosity remain inversely related. While the social settings of the direct religious experiences of blacks and whites apparently differ, there would appear to be no racial differences on the incidence of such experiences. Consequently, it cannot be said that blacks suffer in having an emotional, more direct form of religion. In this regard at least, the stereotype of blacks as more religious is rejected.

*The Ideological Dimension*

Stereotype would also have blacks more conservative in religious ideology, or more sectarian or otherworldly in their religious beliefs. Data for the ideological dimension are from two sets of Gallup survey data. The earlier set was collected in 1957 and subsequently analyzed by Norval Glenn, who began his report with the assumption that "religion can influence and be influenced by power relations and other aspects of social structure [and this] is exemplified by the religion of American Negroes [including] . . . beliefs and practices [which] are, among other things, aids to adaptation to a subordinate status."[25] Concerning ideology, Glenn concludes that "the responses to questions on religious belief indicate a greater tendency for Negroes to be traditional, fundamentalist Christians."[26] Glenn based much of his description of the rural, Southern black upon the earlier, very dated account by Krueger.[27] Glenn notes that cultural lag is reflected in the phenomenon of rural Southern blacks being more conservative in religious ideology. "The religion of rural Southern Negroes is merely the evangelical religion that characterized the American frontier, modified to meet the unique needs of the slaves and freedmen [and] the frontier brand of evangelical Protestantism has generally disappeared among whites as they have become better educated, more sophisticated, and more prosperous, but it has survived in modified and elaborated form among Southern rural Negroes, who have been isolated from the main stream of cultural change and economic advancement."[28]

In his analysis Glenn reports controlling for education, but not for region of the country or size of community of residence. Glenn then traces the changes which have occurred in the religion of urban Negroes, but he continues to hold a belief that black theology is conservative and that blacks interpret the Bible in a literal fashion, characteristic of rural sectarianism.[29] "The religion of urban lower-class Negroes is highly varied, but in general it is much more like the traditional rural Negro religion than like urban middle-class religion. The services generally are again highly emotional, and there is often shouting and singing similar to that in the southern rural churches. With a few exceptions, the lower-class churches and sects are very otherworldly and less concerned with secular affairs than the middle-class churches. Their clergymen are less active in race activities, or not active at all."[30]

The data from the March 1957 Gallup study analyzed by Glenn were reanalyzed for this study. The responses to four items were successfully Guttman scaled (coefficient of reproducibility = .96) to form a measure of the ideological dimension.[31]

The technique used in the analysis of the data, Multiple Classification Analysis, calls for a dichotomized dependent variable or one at the interval level of measurement. Here an ordinal-level measurement is utilized, but it is unidimensional and is shown to have inter-item reliability (and face validity, based on the examination of the items); consequently, it seems permissible to relax somewhat this stringent requirement of interval level measurement for the dependent variable. The effects of the several predictors upon the dependent variable, the ideological dimension of religiosity, using data from 1957, can be seen from Table 3.

Glenn's assessment of the relatively greater sectarianism of black Americans *based on 1957 data*, is basically correct. Sectarianism was

## Table 3

### Effects of Race, Education, Region, and Residence on the Ideological Dimension
### (1957 Data, Protestants Only)

| Predictors | Eta Coefficient[a] | Beta Coefficient[a] |
|---|---|---|
| Race | -.06[b] | -.09 |
| Education | -.15 | -.10 |
| Region | -.28 | -.23 |
| Residence | -.24 | -.20 |

NOTE: N=1,104, R=.357 (d.f.=7).
[a]Unless indicated, all coefficients are significant at the .01 level, using appropriate F tests of significance.
[b]Significant at the .05 level.

especially exhibited by individuals with lower levels of education, from the South, and from smaller communities. The mean value for nonwhites on this scale was 2.86 (adjusted to 2.95), while for whites it was 2.64 (adjusted to 2.63).

A more recent set of data was obtained to examine racial differences on the same dimension. Conducted in June, 1968, this Gallup survey included four items not identical with but closely related to the earlier items.[32] This measure, like its predecessor, is concerned with fundamentalism, or conservative religious ideology.

The index was shown to have high internal consistency.[33] From an examination of the items, it was concluded that the index measures the same dimension of religiosity as that measured by the scale developed from the 1957 data.[34]

Table 4 summarizes the relationships between the various predictors and this measure of the ideological dimension. In comparing the findings of Tables 3 and 4, it can be noted that in 1968 there were no longer significant racial differences on the ideological dimension. For the 104 black Protestants, the mean value of this index ranging from 0 through 4 was 3.30 (adjusted to 3.19), while the mean value for the 949 white Protestants was 2.99 (3.00 adjusted). In other words, after differences in education, region, and

## Table 4

### Effects of Race, Education, Region, and Residence on the Ideological Dimension
### (1968 Data, Protestants Only)

| Predictors | Eta Coefficient | Beta Coefficient |
|---|---|---|
| Race | -.07 | -.04[a] |
| Education | -.16 | -.10 |
| Region | -.21 | -.17 |
| Residence | -.22 | -.18 |

NOTE: N=1,053, R=.296 (d.f.=7).

[a]Not significant at the .05 level, using appropriate F test of significance. Unless indicated, all other coefficients are significant at the .01 level.

residence were controlled, black and white Protestants had similar mean values in this dimension of religiosity. Again, sectarianism was especially high in individuals with lower levels of education, from the South, and from smaller communities, or in individuals not well integrated into the mainstream of American culture. A separate analysis of the black portion of the sample gave coefficients similar in magnitude and direction to those found in Table 4 for the effects of education, region, and residence. (An analysis of racial differences in answers to the two items—life-after-death and the devil—asked in both the 1957 and the 1968 surveys indicated that nonwhites were slightly more likely to endorse the latter item than were whites at both time periods, but the differences lacked significance.)

### The Ritualistic Dimension: Prayer

A third dimension of religiosity concerns ritualism, and here differences for prayer and attendance will be shown separately since the dimension might otherwise mask possible racial differences in devotionalism and associational involvement.

A belief that blacks are more "religious" than whites might include holding that blacks pray more frequently; and this might be coupled with a greater tendency toward otherworldly religion. In

Table 5

Effects of Selected Predictors on the
Frequency of Prayer
(1963 Data, Protestants Only)

| Predictors | Eta Coefficient | Beta Coefficient |
|---|---|---|
| Sex | -.26 | -.26 |
| Age | +.13 | +.14 |
| Race | -.02[a] | -.02[a] |
| Education | +.04[a] | +.04[a] |
| Occupation | +.09 | +.07 |
| Region | -.03[a] | -.05[b] |
| Residence | +.06 | +.06 |

NOTE: N=2,470, R=.309 (d.f.=12).
[a]Not significant at the .05 level, using appropriate F test of significance. Unless indicated, all other coefficients are significant at the .01 level.
[b]Significant at the .05 level.

this section racial differences in frequency of prayer will be examined. It is expected that no differences will be found.

A December 1963 Gallup survey contained an item on prayer: "Do you ever pray? About how often—frequently, occasionally or seldom?" The "yes" responses (but with no answer about regularity) were excluded in the analysis, while "no" responses were lumped with "seldom." Again the analysis is limited to Protestants, since the bulk of black Americans are Protestant and since racial differences in religiosity are being examined.

Table 5 summarizes the effects of various predictors on prayer. Here, sex, age, and occupation have been added to the list of predictors because it was expected that in the ritualistic dimension these additional predictors would provide additional insight.[35] The theoretical reasoning behind the inclusion of these variables was given earlier in this study. Findings concerning possible racial differences in the ritualistic dimension are not changed by the employment of these additional factors.

From an analysis of data collected in 1958 in Detroit, Lenski concluded that only in devotionalism do blacks appear to be more religious than whites. His devotionalism measure was composed of items measuring frequency of prayer and seeking God's will.[36] It might be noted that the latter item is, in part, of a consequential nature. On devotionalism, slightly more than two-thirds of black Protestants ranked high, followed by not quite one-half of white Catholics and not quite one-third of white Protestants.

Here racial differences were not found. Frequency of prayer was positively associated with age and inversely associated with sex (as coded), with females being more likely to turn to prayer. Other coefficients, while significant here, were of lesser magnitude. An analysis of the 641 nonwhites (of these 629 were black) gave coefficients very similar in magnitude and direction except for education which was -.06 (not significant at the .05 level). In sum, the predictor variables act in the same way for whites and non-whites; and there are no racial differences, indicating that blacks are not more religious than whites in this dimension. Blacks cannot be described as being more otherworldly than whites, or more likely to escape from temporal concerns through greater frequency of prayer.

*The Ritualistic Dimension: Church Attendance*

The second aspect of the ritualistic dimension, church attendance, presents us with one crucial problem of measurement, namely, the time period best for ascertaining whether racial differences exist. One escape from this dilemma, which assumes there may be differences during one time period but not during another, is the use of a number of data sets for reanalysis.[37] Generally, white Catholics have the highest attendance, followed by nonwhite Protestants and, finally, by white Protestants. A second strategy is the examination of possible differences in attendance over time; such a trends analysis will be presented in the concluding chapter. Here the findings of three secondary analyses will be examined. The first set of data (and first analysis) concerns recency of attendance. The second and third sets include the more traditional question concerning attendance: "Did you, yourself, happen to attend church in the last 7 days?"

It has been suggested that "Negro religiosity is comparable to that of white Protestants generally," and that "there is yet an extraordinary degree of at least nominal fealty to the church among

*Table 6*

Effects of Race, Education, Region, and Residence
on Church Attendance
(June 1968 Data, Protestants Only)

| Predictors | Eta Coefficient[a] | Beta Coefficient[a] |
|---|---|---|
| Race | -.14 | -.15 |
| Education | +.10 | +.17 |
| Region | -.16 | -.16 |
| Residence | -.08 | -.11 |

NOTE: N=1,046, R=.259 (d.f.=7).
[a]Using the appropriate F tests of significance, all coefficients are significant at the .01 level.

blacks."[38] Lenski reported that nearly 40 percent of his black sample attended worship services every Sunday and only 5 percent never went to church. Attendance was higher for middle-class than for working-class black Protestants.[39] Babchuk and Thompson noted that only 12.5 percent of the blacks in their Lincoln, Nebraska sample were not religiously affiliated; however, they attribute church attendance on the part of blacks as release from a "restrictive social environment."[40]

If there is greater loyalty to the black church, we would expect racial differences on the attendance variable, with blacks being more likely to report higher attendance. More frequent attendance on the part of blacks would be interpreted not as an escapist religious orientation, but as involvement in the black community. This subject will be further discussed in the concluding chapter.

A June 1968 Gallup survey included the question "When was the last time you have been to church?" This was coded as: seldom or never, 1-12 months ago, 3-4 weeks ago, 2-3 weeks ago, 1-2 weeks ago, and last Sunday. The data have been subjected to Multiple Classification Analysis, even though the dependent variable is not at the interval level of measurement. The effects of race, education, region, and residence on recency of attendance are shown in Table 6. The analysis is limited to Protestants. Attendance (ranging from 0,

**Church Attendance    75**

Table 7

Effects of Selected Predictors on Attendance
(December 1963 Data, Protestants Only)

| Predictors | Eta Coefficient | Beta Coefficient |
|---|---|---|
| Sex | -.16 | -.16 |
| Age | +.08 | +.08 |
| Race | -.01[a] | -.06 |
| Education | +.08 | +.07 |
| Occupation | +.10 | +.10 |
| Region | -.12 | -.12 |
| Residence | -.04[b] | -.05[b] |

NOTE: N=2,574, R=.248 (d.f.=12).
[a]Not significant at the .05 level, using appropriate F test of significance. Unless indicated, all other coefficients are significant at the .01 level.
[b]Significant at the .05 level.

or never, to 5, or last Sunday) was inversely related with race (coded black-white), region (coded South-non-South) and residence (coded nonmetropolitan-metropolitan) and positively associated with education. Residential differences were found here, possibly because subtle differences in recency of attendance were tapped by the measure, rather than attendance during the past week. A separate analysis of the black respondents here also indicated significant (.01 level) differences by residence.

Next let us turn to the presentation of results from two analyses of responses concerning attendance in the past seven days, using Gallup surveys conducted in December 1963 and May 1969 (two separate surveys in May 1969 are pooled here). As in the analysis of possible racial differences on frequency of prayer (the first aspect of the ritualistic dimension), the predictor variables sex, age, and occupation (as well as race, education, region, and residence), were included in the analysis of the 1963 data.[41] Table 7 shows the effects of these predictors on attendance in the past seven days. Without controls, there were no racial differences in attendance (eta = -.01), but with the introduction of the controls, nonwhites (of whom the great majority are black) were more likely to report

## Table 8

### Effects of Selected Predictors on Attendance
### (December 1963 Data, Nonwhites Only)

| Predictors | Eta Coefficient | Beta Coefficient |
|---|---|---|
| Sex | -.16 | -.17 |
| Age | +.31 | +.34 |
| Education | +.09[a] | +.13 |
| Occupation | +.16 | +.11 |
| Region | -.06[a] | -.01[a] |
| Residence | -.12 | -.05[a] |

NOTE: N=518, R=.370 (d.f.=11).

[a]Not significant at the .05 level, using appropriate F test of significance. Unless indicated, all other coefficients are significant at the .01 level.

attending during the past seven days. As expected higher attendance was positively associated with age, education, and occupation and was inversely associated with sex (coded female-male), region (South-non-South) and residential size. It should be noted that residential differences here, while significant, were slight.[42]

The same coefficients (with the exception of race) are shown for nonwhites in Table 8. The directions of the coefficients are the same as in the previous table, although several coefficients do not reach significance, due in part to the small sample size. For nonwhites, there are no differences in attendance by region. On the other hand, the coefficient for the effect of age was .34 (for the entire sample it was .08). Because of possible interaction effects, the analysis was rerun for white Protestants; in general the coefficients were of the same magnitude and in the same direction, except for age. For white Protestants there were no significant differences in attendance by age. Differences in attendance by age category are shown for nonwhites in Table 9. Attendance is especially high for nonwhites 45 and older. Whether this portends a decline in the black church in the coming decades cannot be answered here. This may be the case, partially because of urban migration by younger individuals and the greater effect of urbanward migration on children of migrants. But

## Table 9

### Church Attendance by Age
### (December 1963 Data, Nonwhites Only)

| Age Categories | N | Percentage in each Category | Unadjusted Percentage Attending | Adjusted Percentage Attending[a] |
|---|---|---|---|---|
| 34 and under | 172 | 33.2 | 32.0 | 27.1 |
| 35-44 | 164 | 31.7 | 26.8 | 29.0 |
| 45-54 | 71 | 13.7 | 63.4 | 61.9 |
| 55 and over | 111 | 21.4 | 58.6 | 63.5 |

[a]Adjusted percentage controlling for the effects of sex, age, education, occupation, region, and residence.

more likely it is simply a part of black culture that people turn with greater interest to church matters as they become older.

For a more recent set of data, two surveys completed in May, 1969 were pooled. Again the analysis is limited to Protestants. The effects of race, education, region, and residence on church attendance can be observed in Table 10. There are significant racial differences, with blacks more likely to report attendance in the past seven days than whites. Again education and attendance are positively related. For these data, however, there are no significant differences in attendance by region or residence.

So far in our examination of possible racial differences in the various dimensions of religiosity, results have been as predicted: no black-white differences were found on the experiential and ideological (1968 data) dimensions and blacks did not turn with greater frequency to prayer. Each of these dimensions could be interpreted to be part of emotional, otherworldly religion; and thus the discovery that racial differences were absent meant that we could reject the stereotype of the black American as having a penchant for an emotional, otherworldly religion. On the other hand, significant differences were found in church attendance, with blacks showing more fealty to the church than whites. Greater attendance on the part of blacks has been interpreted as not necessarily indicating greater receptivity to otherworldly religion but rather reflecting

*Table 10*

## Effects of Race, Education, Region, and Residence on Attendance
### (May 1969 Data, Protestants Only)

| Predictors | Eta Coefficient | Beta Coefficient |
|---|---|---|
| Race | −.08 | −.10 |
| Education | +.14 | +.16 |
| Region | −.03[a] | −.04[a] |
| Residence | +.04[a] | −.01[a] |

NOTE: N=1,961; R=.165 (d.f.=7).
[a]Not significant at the .05 level, using appropriate F test of significance. Unless indicated, all other coefficients are significant at the .01 level.

loyalty to the church as one of the central institutions of the black community and as an integral part of the cohesive community. More will be said on this subject when the trends analysis is presented.

### The Intellectual Dimension

The remaining dimension concerns the intellectual variable, or religious knowledge. This dimension is of the least theoretical interest to us, but it might be argued that blacks, who would be more likely according to stereotype to evince an otherworldly interest, should score lower on religious knowledge since a cognitive orientation to religion might be counter to one that is emotional. Again no significant differences by race are expected.

An earlier study (Gallup, November 1954) provided data for ascertaining nonwhite-white differences in this dimension. Individuals low in religious knowledge were familiar with three or less of seven items calling for religious knowledge.[43]

Table 11 indicates the effects of race, education, region, and residence on the intellectual dimension for Protestants only. There were no racial differences. Regional and residential differences, while significant, were minimal. Religious knowledge, not too surprisingly, was positively related with education. It can be said, at least, that

*Table 11*

Effects of Race, Education, Region, and
Residence on the Intellectual Dimension
(November 1954 Data, Protestants Only)

| Predictors | Eta Coefficient | Beta Coefficient |
|---|---|---|
| Race | +.03[a] | +.00[a] |
| Education | +.26 | +.26 |
| Region | −.08 | −.07[b] |
| Residence | −.06[b] | −.07[b] |

NOTE: N=1,015; R=.270 (d.f.=7).

[a]Not significant at the .05 level, using appropriate F test of significance. Unless indicated, all other coefficients are significant at the .01 level.

[b]Significant at the .05 level.

the finding of no racial differences does nothing to substantiate the stereotyped view that blacks are more otherworldly in their religious orientation.

### Conclusions

From a comparison of data gathered in a nationwide survey of anti-Semitism, Gary Marx has noted that there are few differences between whites and blacks with regard to religious outlook. "When the various dimensions of religiosity are examined, holding the effect of education and region constant, Negroes appear as significantly more religious *only* with respect to the subjective importance assigned to religion. In the North whites were more likely to attend church at least once a week than were Negroes, while in the South rates of attendance were the same. . . . any assertions about the greater religiosity of Negroes relative to whites are unwarranted unless one specifies the dimension of religiosity being measured."[44]

We have not had the chance to compare the races with respect to the saliency of religion for each. We would expect that blacks would be more likely than whites to check that religion is important to them personally; this statement is speculative, however, and based in part on Marx's finding. There would be theoretical ground for the prediction, namely, the importance of the black church to the black community as an institution linked with the cohesiveness of the community and as one of the central institutions of the community over time. Marx's comment seemingly indicates that there are no overall black-white differences in two of three dimensions (attendance, orthodoxy, and saliency) included in his interview schedule; but we do not know whether the introduction of additional controls (for example, age, sex, and residential background) would have diminished the relationship between race and saliency. Furthermore, his variables are related to only two of Glock's five variables, and his sample is drawn altogether from metropolitan areas.

Let us examine the findings reported in this chapter. By the discovery of no racial differences in the reported occurrences of religious experience, in the frequency of prayer, in the holding of conservative religious beliefs, or in levels of religious knowledge, the thesis was supported that blacks are not more likely than whites to subscribe to an emotional, otherworldly religious orientation. The religious part of the stereotype that blacks are otherworldly and thus not concerned with temporal problems must be rejected. In the next chapter we turn to an assessment of the second characteristic (that blacks are not concerned with temporal problems) by focusing on black expectations for their ministers and churches in terms of protest and making pronouncements. Through such an examination we also indirectly examine the relationship between religiosity and civil rights militancy. A more direct assessment of this relationship will be made later in this study.

# 5:

# Religiosity and Militancy:
# An Indirect Examination
# of a Relationship

The most recent analysis of the possible consequences of black religion has been completed by Gary Marx, who analyzed the relationship between religiosity and militancy. His argument will be examined in greater detail in the next chapter, but it should be noted that he views religion as sedating, rather than stimulating, the drive toward radicalism among the black masses.[1] His conclusion is in a long tradition which views black religion as "a safety valve where thwarted desires and emotions may be freely vented."[2] Yet Marx notes that literature identifying black religion as the source of race protest can be found.[3]

In this chapter we will examine Gallup data for black-white differences in protest attitudes. Because we reject the belief that black religion is sectarian, we generally expect to find that black Americans are more approving of ministers being involved in protest actions and the churches speaking out on political and social questions. Such findings would be more startling than one might first believe since stereotypes would characterize blacks as being otherworldly in religious views; and since sectarian individuals do not desire protest or social concern on the part of their ministers and churches, blacks should generally not favor a militant stance on the part of the religious institution. The secondary analyses to be reported in this chapter will be concerned with racial comparisons of expectations in regard to the role of the church and ministers in addressing social problems. The view coupling black religiosity with lack of militancy will thus be indirectly examined in this chapter.

Here we will examine, in order, the involuntary attitude toward church participation, the church acting as an agency of social control, and receptivity toward protest ministers. The first two items are concerned with attitudes toward church participation and expectations that the church will act at least to some degree as an agency of social control. The finding that blacks are more likely than whites to embrace a more vigorous role for the church as an institution claiming their allegiance and issuing pronouncements will make more acceptable the thesis that participation in the black church can imply a desire for a social protest role on the part of the church and that such a role is compatible with a churchlike orientation.

### The Black Church As Semi-Involuntary

The thesis is developed in *Black Church in America* that the black church, especially in the more rural areas, is a semi-involuntary, communal organization and that the black church contributes to the communal and personal organization of black Americans.[4] Such a view would be linked with the finding of greater fealty to the church on the part of blacks than whites, as evidenced by more recent attendance. In the last chapter the finding of more frequent attendance by blacks was reported, and it is suggested that differences in attendance between black and white Protestants vary over time, with greater attendance by blacks especially pronounced prior to and after the period of time when integration was felt to be occurring. The analysis of these data will be presented in the concluding chapter.

The black church as a central community institution can more easily claim the allegiance of community members than can the white church, which is in competition with a proliferation of community associations. Frazier observed that among lower-class black Americans "there is little associational life and the churches of all types represent . . . the main form of organized social life."[5] Yet, because of changes in the class structure and urbanization, Frazier believed that the church was declining, both as a retreat from the larger world and as a vehicle of social control.[6]

*Table 12*

Effects of Race, Education, Region, and
Residence on the Voluntary Characteristic
(March 1957 Data, Protestants Only)

| Predictors | Eta Coefficient | Beta Coefficient |
|---|---|---|
| Race | +.12 | +.11 |
| Education | +.13 | +.10[b] |
| Region | +.14 | +.11 |
| Residence | +.05[a] | +.05[a] |

NOTE: N=1,080; R=.195 (d.f.=7).
[a]Not significant at the .05 level, using appropriate F test of significance. Unless indicated, all other coefficients are significant at the .01 level.
[b]Significant at the .05 level.

The virtual necessity of belonging to and attending church should be primarily a rural, conservative phenomenon. Yet, on the other hand, there is little reason to expect the rural church to be strongest in impoverished areas; indeed, the converse is true, as noted earlier.

Two Gallup surveys (March 1957 and December 1963) included the question: "Do you think a person can be a Christian if he doesn't go to church?" The question is, of course, linked with conservative religious ideology, but at the same time it also captures the involuntary characteristic, namely, that a religious person is duty-bound to participate in the religious organization. The first set of data was collected prior to the period when integration seemed more than just a dream, while the second set of data was collected when it was felt that assimilation was a viable process. If the black church is linked with black community cohesion and ethnogenesis rather than with the process of assimilation into the larger society, and if the question can be said to test the involuntary characteristic, then we might expect blacks to be more likely than whites to subscribe to this involuntary expectation for the first data set but not for the second set.[7] It is unfortunate that we do not have the responses to the same question for 1968 or 1969. A finding that there were no racial differences in the responses to this question in

*Table 13*

Effects of Race, Education, Region, and
Residence on the Voluntary Characteristic
(December 1963 Data, Protestants Only)

| Predictors | Eta Coefficient | Beta Coefficient |
|---|---|---|
| Race | +.02[a] | +.01[a] |
| Education | +.09 | +.07 |
| Region | +.14 | +.12 |
| Residence | +.06 | +.04[b] |

NOTE: N=2,857; R=.151 (d.f.=7).
[a]Not significant at the .05 level, using appropriate F test of significance. Unless indicated, all other coefficients are significant at the .01 level.
[b]Significant at the .05 level.

1968 or 1969 might indicate that the item is more closely associated with conservative ideology than with an involuntary attitude per se. It should be remembered that in the last chapter the finding was presented that racial differences in religious ideology had apparently disappeared by the late 1960s. On the other hand, a finding that blacks are more likely to embrace the involuntary response might be interpreted as a return to greater fealty to the church. A search of the file of questions employed by the Gallup Organization indicated, however, that the question was not repeated after 1963.

Table 12 summarizes the relationships between the four predictors generally employed in analyses of racial differences in religiosity and the item, coded as no-yes, or involuntary-voluntary. The data here are from March 1957. Whites, individuals with more education, and nonsoutherners were more likely to give the *voluntary* response. The differences by residence were not significant, perhaps partially because the sample was so small. Of the 136 nonwhite Protestants, 71.3 percent (72.0 percent adjusted for the effects of the other predictors) gave the voluntary response, compared to 84.9 percent (84.7 percent adjusted) of the 944 white Protestants.

The results of the reanalysis of the more recent data (December

1963) are shown in Table 13. While there were significant residential differences (note the larger sample size and the fact that the magnitude of the beta coefficient for residence did not increase in Table 13), there were no racial differences here. For nonwhites considered separately, there were no residential differences (the data are not shown). The date of this second survey must be remembered, as blacks, and Americans generally, believed that the period of integration had come. Probably at this period black institutions were generally waning.[8]

The Church and Social Control

Related to the involuntary characteristic is the view that the church should "speak its mind" on social evils of the society. Through its pronouncements the church acts as an agency of social control. Here might be located the seeds of the church's involvement in social reform and even in protest for civil rights. Yet an affirmative answer to a question about approval of the church's involvement in social reform might be related to a more conservative orientation with regard to religious ideology, because such a response might imply approval of church interference with individual freedom, especially in matters of importance to the "Puritan ethic" (for example, drinking alcoholic beverages).[9] That is, the individual replying positively to a question about the church taking social stands might as easily take a conservative stance in question of personal ethics. An older, liberal orientation divorced the church and the making of public policy because of a fear that the church would attempt to abridge freedoms of individual behavior. In conclusion, the role of the church as challenger of traditional social relationships, especially in regard to race, might receive impetus from a more conservative mechanism which includes the church's regulation of social conduct. In such a way, church involvement might be linked with feelings of protest, especially on the part of minority group members.

Again we turn to two Gallup surveys, and here we have a greater span of time—March 1957 to February 1968. The argument has been developed that "the power of the black church as an involuntary association has lessened" and that "there appears to be at this time an increasing number of black ministers who realize that the black

*Table 14*

Effects of Selected Predictors on the Attitude that
the Church Should Speak out on Social Issues
(March 1957 and February 1968 Data, All Respondents)

| Predictors | Eta Coefficient | Beta Coefficient |
|---|---|---|
| Sex | -.10 | -.09 |
| Age | -.11 | -.10 |
| Race | -.13 | -.14 |
| Education | +.07[b] | +.07[b] |
| Occupation | +.03[a] | +.06 |
| Region | -.04[a] | -.01[a] |
| Residence | -.04[b] | -.07 |
| Time of study | -.07 | -.06 |

NOTE: N=2,457; R=.217 (d.f.=13)

[a]Not significant at the .05 level, using appropriate F test of significance. Unless indicated, all other coefficients are significant at the .01 level.
[b]Significant at the .05 level.

church must become a voluntary association with goals oriented to ensuring equality, justice, love, and perhaps even the Christianizing of the white society."[10] Such a transition from semi-involuntary to voluntary membership ties, with an organizational goal of more concern for justice and for black community development, should be aided by the complementary characteristics of the church as an agency for social control and for social prophecy. Here might be the foundation for a dual orientation of religion, as providing comfort and a conservative spirit as well as calling for radical reform.

The question can again be raised concerning who would expect churches to "keep out of political matters" and who would expect them to "express their views on day-to-day social and political questions." The wording of the item—"Should the churches keep out of political matters or should they express their views on day-to-day social and political questions?"—could include a wide spectrum of church involvement, from acting as an agent of social control to serving as a radical challenger of the structure and norms of white society.[11]

*Table 15*

Effects of Selected Predictors on the Attitude that
the Church Should Speak Out on Social Issues
(March 1957 and February 1968 Data, White Respondents)

| Predictors | Eta Coefficient | Beta Coefficient |
|---|---|---|
| Sex | -.09 | -.08 |
| Age | -.10 | -.09 |
| Education | .08[b] | .08[b] |
| Occupation | +.05 | +.05 |
| Region | -.01[a] | -.00[a] |
| Residence | -.05 | -.06 |
| Time of study | -.08 | -.08 |

NOTE: N=2,226; R=.173 (d.f.=12).

[a]Not significant at the .05 level, using appropriate F test of significance. Unless indicated, all other coefficients are significant at the .01 level.

[b]The direction of the relationship is not specified; percentages by category are shown in Table 17.

Table 14 indicates the effects of several predictors on attitude toward the church speaking out on social and political issues. Females, younger respondents, nonwhites, residents of smaller communities, white-collar workers, and the more highly educated were more likely to express the view that the church should address its attention to social and political issues. Of greatest interest is the fact that 68.4 percent (69.5 percent adjusted) of the 231 nonwhites compared to 46.4 percent (both unadjusted and adjusted) of the whites favored the social prophecy role for the church. This finding clearly contradicts the stereotype of blacks as being otherworldly in religion, desiring their church to stay out of temporal matters. For the entire sample, there was a decrease in the percentage of individuals feeling that the church should speak out on social ills when responses were compared over time (1957 and 1968).

Tables 15 and 16 present the coefficients for whites and nonwhites separately, because here clearly interaction is occurring. For example, by specifying race, different trends over time appear, and this finding is of crucial importance to the study.

*Table 16*

Effects of Selected Predictors on the Attitude that
the Church Should Speak out on Social Issues
(March 1957 and February 1968 Data, Nonwhite Respondents)

| Predictors | Eta Coefficient | Beta Coefficient |
|---|---|---|
| Sex | -.24 | -.24 |
| Age | -.20[b] | -.23 |
| Education | -.07[a] | -.24 |
| Occupation | +.10[a] | +.16 |
| Region | -.15[b] | -.06[a] |
| Residence | -.11[a] | -.06[a] |
| Time of study | +.08[a] | +.13[b] |

NOTE: N=231; R=.336 (d.f.=12).
[a]Not significant at the .05 level, using appropriate F test of significance.
Unless indicated, all other coefficients are significant at the .01 level.
[b]Significant at the .05 level.

Tables 17 and 18 summarize the data, giving percentages by categories of each predictor listed in Tables 15 and 16. As can be seen from Table 18, there was an inverse relationship between education and preference for the church speaking out on the part of nonwhites. Yet it is that group which, according to stereotype, should be most otherworldly in religious orientation that here most desires the church's involvement in social and political concerns. Over two-thirds of nonwhite respondents with an eighth-grade education or less felt the church should speak out on social and political issues, in comparison to less than one-half of the nonwhite respondents with some college or more (the other figures can be seen in Table 18). Younger respondents, both white and nonwhite, favored the involved role, but the differences in response between old and young were greater for nonwhites than for whites.

Whites increasingly are less likely to desire the church's involvement in social and political matters, while nonwhites increasingly are more likely to desire this involvement. Of the whites surveyed in 1957, 50.2 percent desired involvement, compared to 42.3 percent of those interviewed in 1968.[12] Of the nonwhites polled in 1957,

## Table 17

### Percentage Believing that the Church Should Speak Out on Social and Political Issues, by Selected Predictors (March 1957 and February 1968 Data, White Respondents)

| Predictors | N | Percentage in each Category | Percentage Giving Positive Response | Adjusted Percentage[a] |
|---|---|---|---|---|
| **Sex** | | | | |
| Female | 1,116 | 50.1 | 50.9 | 50.6 |
| Male | 1,110 | 49.9 | 41.8 | 42.2 |
| **Age** | | | | |
| 34 and under | 710 | 31.9 | 52.5 | 52.3 |
| 35-44 | 558 | 25.1 | 47.1 | 46.7 |
| 45-54 | 528 | 23.7 | 43.0 | 43.1 |
| 55 and over | 430 | 19.3 | 39.3 | 40.4 |
| **Education** | | | | |
| 8th grade or less | 440 | 19.8 | 42.7 | 45.4 |
| 9th-11th grade | 468 | 21.0 | 49.6 | 49.4 |
| High school diploma | 829 | 37.2 | 43.2 | 42.2 |
| Some college or more | 489 | 22.0 | 51.9 | 51.6 |
| **Occupation** | | | | |
| Blue-collar | 1,334 | 59.9 | 44.5 | 44.3 |
| White-collar | 892 | 40.1 | 49.2 | 49.5 |
| **Region** | | | | |
| South | 576 | 25.9 | 47.0 | 46.8 |
| Non-South | 1,650 | 74.1 | 46.1 | 46.3 |
| **Residence** | | | | |
| Nonmetropolitan | 1,102 | 49.5 | 49.0 | 49.6 |
| Metropolitan | 1,124 | 50.5 | 43.8 | 43.2 |
| **Time of study** | | | | |
| March 1957 | 1,155 | 51.9 | 50.2 | 50.2 |
| February 1968 | 1,071 | 48.1 | 42.2 | 42.3 |

[a]The percentage is adjusted for the effects of all other predictors listed in the table.

*Table 18*

Percentage Believing that the Church Should Speak Out
on Social and Political Issues, by Selected Predictors
(March 1957 and February 1968 Data, Nonwhite Respondents)

| Predictors | N | Percentage in each Category | Percentage Giving Positive Response | Adjusted Percentage[a] |
|---|---|---|---|---|
| Sex | | | | |
| Female | 113 | 48.9 | 79.6 | 80.0 |
| Male | 118 | 51.1 | 57.6 | 57.3 |
| Age | | | | |
| 34 and under | 83 | 35.9 | 74.7 | 76.9 |
| 35-44 | 66 | 28.6 | 74.2 | 73.9 |
| 45-54 | 44 | 19.0 | 63.6 | 62.2 |
| 55 and over | 38 | 16.5 | 50.0 | 39.5 |
| Education | | | | |
| 8th grade or less | 84 | 36.4 | 69.0 | 79.6 |
| 9th-11th grade | 65 | 28.1 | 69.2 | 71.0 |
| High school diploma | 49 | 21.2 | 71.4 | 59.8 |
| Some college or more | 33 | 14.3 | 60.6 | 47.6 |
| Occupation | | | | |
| Blue-collar | 193 | 83.5 | 66.3 | 65.0 |
| White-collar | 38 | 16.5 | 78.9 | 85.5 |
| Region | | | | |
| South | 92 | 39.8 | 77.2 | 72.1 |
| Non-South | 139 | 60.2 | 62.6 | 66.0 |
| Residence | | | | |
| Nonmetropolitan | 61 | 26.4 | 77.0 | 73.0 |
| Metropolitan | 170 | 73.6 | 65.3 | 66.8 |
| Time of study | | | | |
| March 1957 | 136 | 58.9 | 65.4 | 63.3 |
| February 1968 | 95 | 41.1 | 72.6 | 75.6 |

[a]The percentage is adjusted for the effects of all other predictors listed in the table.

63.3 percent favored involvement, compared to 75.6 percent of those surveyed in 1968.

In summary, using the full set of predictors because our interest has shifted from racial differences in dimensions of religiosity to racial differences in attitudes toward protest, we compared the attitudes of whites and nonwhites on the question of whether the church should speak out on social and political issues. Catholics were not excluded from the analysis since the dependent variable did not concern a dimension of religiosity. Nonwhites were more likely than whites to desire such involvement and there was an increase over time in the percent of nonwhites who desired involvement, while there was a decrease for whites. It is clear then, that the notion that blacks are more likely to be sectarian and thus reject the involvement of the church in temporal matters, must again be dismissed. Furthermore, it was precisely that group of nonwhites who should most dislike involvement, according to the stereotype, who were in favor of it; this group consisted of the respondents at the lower levels of education. In the previous chapter we reported that while blacks were more fundamentalist than whites in 1957, by 1968 such differences had disappeared. Here we have observed an increasing desire for the church to be involved in temporal matters, or a trend away from otherworldly religion. The observer might well reflect that these two trends could be related. In the next chapter we will examine directly the relationship between religiosity and militancy.

### Attitude toward the March on Washington

Data were available for three questions about receptivity toward protesting ministers. A Gallup survey of August, 1963, asked the question: "Have you heard or read about the proposed mass civil rights rally to be held in Washington, D. C. on August 28? What are your feelings about this?" Reactions were coded as unfavorable or favorable (as well as undesignated and no opinion, which were deleted in the analysis). Stereotype would hold that rural blacks, particularly, would be unfavorable to the rally, since ministers were to be involved and since rural blacks would have an otherworldly religious orientation. An analysis of racial and residential differences might shed light here on the presumed inverse relationship between

*Table 19*

Effects of Selected Predictors on Attitude toward
the March on Washington
(August 1963 Data, All Respondents)

| Predictors | *Eta* Coefficient | *Beta* Coefficient |
|---|---|---|
| Sex | −.09 | −.06 |
| Age | −.18 | −.14 |
| Race | −.52 | −.51 |
| Education | −.14 | −.04[a] |
| Occupation | −.08 | +.04[b] |
| Region | +.07 | +.10 |
| Residence | +.14 | +.02[a] |

NOTE: N=1,652; R=.545 (d.f.=12).
[a]Not significant at the .05 level, using appropriate F test of significance. Unless indicated, all other coefficients are significant at the .01 level.
[b]Significant at the .05 level.

religiosity and militancy. First, racial differences will be examined. Table 19 indicates the effects of selected predictor variables on attitude toward the march.

Of the 250 blacks whose responses were analyzed, 85.2 percent (84.0 percent adjusted) approved of the march, compared to 19.5 percent (19.8 percent adjusted) of the 1402 whites. Considering that the march had a large contingent of clergymen, there is little doubt that blacks approved of church leaders being involved in civil rights activities, here measured by the march on Washington. We are assuming, of course, that blacks knew that clergy would be deeply involved in the march on Washington.

Comparable coefficients for blacks are presented in Table 20. In comparing the coefficients in Tables 19 and 20 it can be seen that clear interaction effects are present. Of the 136 black females, 91.9 percent (94.1 percent adjusted) favored the march, compared to 77.2 percent (74.6 percent adjusted) of the 114 black males. Non-southerners were more likely to favor the march than southerners. Of the 90 black southerners, 84.4 percent (76.2 percent adjusted) endorsed the march, compared to 85.6 percent (90.3 percent ad-

## Table 20

### Effects of Selected Predictors on Attitude toward the March on Washington
### (August 1963 Data, Black Respondents)

| Predictors | Eta Coefficient | Beta Coefficient |
|---|---|---|
| Sex | −.21 | −.27 |
| Age | +.14[a] | +.14[a] |
| Education | +.10[a] | +.12[a] |
| Occupation | −.04[a] | −.10[a] |
| Region | +.02[a] | +.19 |
| Residence | −.18 | −.28 |

NOTE: N=250; R=.326 (d.f.=11).
[a]Not significant at the .05 level, using appropriate F test of significance. Unless indicated, all other coefficients are significant at the .01 level.

justed of the 160 nonsouthern blacks. There were also residential differences on this variable for blacks. Of the 40 nonmetropolitan black respondents, all favored the march, compared to 82.4 percent (81.9 percent adjusted) of the 210 metropolitan black respondents. A view of rural residents as being more passive or as being otherworldly and less militant cannot be entertained here for blacks.[13] In sum, blacks were more likely than whites to support a protest role. This conclusion might seem without significance in that blacks might be expected to support problack protest, but the fact that they supported a march involving clergymen is evidence against the stereotype that black religion is sectarian and thus, where religious matters are involved, blacks take an otherworldly stance.

### Attitude toward Clergy Protesting

A more direct question about clergy protest in civil rights activities was included in a March 1965, Gallup survey. Here interviewees were asked "How would you feel about clergymen in your own church taking part in protest marches on civil rights issues. Would you approve or disapprove of this?" Note the relevancy of this ques-

*Table 21*

Effects of Selected Predictors on Attitude toward Clergy Protesting
(March 1965 Data, All Respondents)

| Predictors | Eta Coefficient | Beta Coefficient |
|---|---|---|
| Sex | -.09 | -.08 |
| Age | -.12 | -.07 |
| Race | -.38 | -.37 |
| Education | +.16 | +.13 |
| Occupation | +.02[a] | +.01[a] |
| Income | +.08 | +.07 |
| Region | +.18 | +.18 |
| Residence | +.20 | +.06 |

NOTE: N=2,478; R=.472 (d.f.=16).

[a]Not significant at the .05 level, using appropriate F test of significance. Unless indicated, all other coefficients are significant at the .01 level.

tion—it centers on the ministers in their own denomination. Again, the stereotype of black religion as sectarian (or with ministers expected to reject temporal concerns) is on trial here. The effects of selected predictors on approval of clergy being involved in protest marches are shown in Table 21.

Income has been added here since a question concerning family income was available for this analysis and since it provides additional insight concerning the dependent variable. Like education, it is positively related to receptivity to clergy protesting. A separate analysis of black respondents gave negligible results because of the small sample size; of all the variables, only education proved significant. For the entire sample, there were startling racial differences. Of the 273 black respondents, 88.3 percent (88.0 percent adjusted) replied affirmatively, compared to 30.4 percent (30.5 percent adjusted) of the 2,205 white respondents. These racial differences seem impressive in that the stereotype of black religiosity as otherworldly would not have so high a percentage of blacks being in favor of a protest role on the part of ministers.

As can be seen from the table, approval of protest activities on the part of ministers varies positively with social class (income and

Table 22

Effects of Selected Predictors on Positive Feeling
about Martin Luther King
(May 1963 and May 1965 Data, All Respondents)

| Predictors | Eta Coefficient | Beta Coefficient |
|---|---|---|
| Sex | +.02[a] | +.01[a] |
| Age | -.19 | -.11 |
| Race | -.50 | -.54 |
| Education | +.13 | +.13 |
| Occupation | +.02[a] | +.04[a] |
| Income | +.07 | +.06 |
| Region | +.19 | +.23 |
| Residence | +.22 | +.07 |
| Time of study | +.09 | +.06 |

NOTE: N=5,771; R=.616 (d.f.=17).
[a]Not significant at the .05 level, using appropriate F test of significance. Unless indicated, all other coefficients are significant at the .01 level.

education and positively with size of population of place of residence. Nonsouthern respondents were more likely than southern respondents to favor protest. The most striking difference here is racial identification. What is important is that black ministers are expected to be concerned with racial matters calling for militancy on their part. Their ministerial style is not to be a merely comforting one, serving laity with otherworldly interests.

### Attitude toward Martin Luther King, Jr.

Finally let us turn to a question concerning approval or disapproval of Martin Luther King, Jr. The item, included in Gallup surveys of May 1963, and May 1965, was as follows: "Here's an interesting experiment. . . . You notice that the 10 boxes on this card go from the HIGHEST POSITION OF PLUS 5—or someone you like very much—all the way down to the LOWEST POSITION OF MINUS 5—or someone you dislike very much. Please tell me how far up the scale or how far down the scale you would rate the following

Table 23

Effects of Selected Predictors on Positive Feeling
about Martin Luther King
(May 1963 and May 1965 Data, Black Respondents)

| Predictors | Eta Coefficient | Beta Coefficient |
|---|---|---|
| Sex | +.12 | +.10 |
| Age | +.15 | .15[c] |
| Education | +.10[b] | +.12 |
| Occupation | −.01[a] | −.10 |
| Income | +.25 | +.14 |
| Region | +.22 | +.08 |
| Residence | +.32 | +.24 |
| Time of study | +.02[a] | +.00[a] |

NOTE: N=752; R=.393 (d.f.=16).
[a]Not significant at the .05 level, using appropriate F test of significance. Unless indicated, all other coefficients are significant at the .01 level.
[b]Significant at the .05 level.
[c]The direction of the relationship is not specified here; means by age category are reported in the text.

men. . . . " In both surveys the name of the Reverend Martin Luther King, Jr., was included in the lists. In a reanalysis the data were reformated to range from 0 (minus 5) to 9 (plus 5) and an interval level of measurement was assumed to be present.

The same predictors as those employed in the previous analysis were used, except that time of study (1963 versus 1965) was added. More likely to approve of King were respondents who were younger, black, with more education and with greater family income, non-southern, and metropolitan in residence; and respondents were more positive about King in the later survey. These coefficients for the entire sample are shown in Table 22. From a comparison of Tables 22 and 23 (the latter table presents the coefficients for the black respondents), it is apparent that there is interaction occurring, with some changes in the effects of the predictor variables, depending upon the race of the respondent. Among black respondents, males, respondents reporting the head of the family as a blue-collar worker, and younger (but not the youngest age category) respondents were more likely to favor King. For blacks there were no differences by time of study, and region had less effect than it did for the entire sample.

For the entire sample, there was a clear, inverse relationship between age and favoring King, with the adjusted means being 4.18 (age 34 and under), 3.73 (35-44), 3.59 (45-54), and 2.11 (55 and over). For the black respondents, however, the relationship was somewhat curvilinear, with the adjusted means being, in order, 7.77, 8.49, 8.13, and 7.95. It is most likely that the youngest blacks in the sample felt King was not oriented enough to black power or was not militant enough. A separate analysis of the 1965 data indicated a clear, inverse relationship between age and approval of the Black Muslims, a finding that lends support to this interpretation.

*Conclusions*

In this chapter black-white differences in attitudes toward protest were examined. It was found that black Americans are more approving of ministers being involved in protest actions and of the churches speaking out on political and social questions. Since stereotype would have blacks more sectarian, blacks thus should prefer their ministers and churches to keep out of protest activities. The data show that this is not the case, again indicating that the idea of blacks as basically otherworldly, or not concerned with temporal matters, must be rejected. From an analysis of data on the involuntary attitude (i.e., the feeling that church attendance is a requirement) and on the attitude toward the church's speaking out on political and social issues, it was concluded that an involved role on the part of the church is compatible with a conservative theological orientation (a conservative orientation is not necessarily coupled with sectarianism).

Blacks were more likely than whites to favor the church's speaking out on social and political questions. Blacks increasingly favored this while whites decreasingly favored it over the time period of 1957 to 1968. For the skeptic who might interpret our findings to mean simply that blacks are more likely than whites to favor the extension of civil rights, it should be noted that the question concerning the church's speaking out on social and political matters was phrased in general terms, not being limited to racial or civil rights issues. We cannot agree with the skeptic, then, that black militancy in the religious context stems only from self-interest and as such is race issue specific.

Three questions dealt with receptivity toward protest ministers. On all questions—opinion on the march on Washington, receptivity toward the idea of clergymen from their own churches protesting, and feeling about Martin Luther King, Jr.—blacks were more likely than whites to give a militant response, that is, to favor the protest role for ministers and to favor King.

In sum, blacks were more likely than whites to embrace a more vigorous role for the church as an agency claiming their allegiance and as an institution making pronouncements and taking a protest stance. This finding gives support to the thesis that participation in the black church might well imply the desire for a social protest role on the part of the church and that such a role would be compatible with a churchlike orientation.

# 6:

# Religiosity and Militancy:
# A Direct Examination

In the introductory chapter it was noted that there has been little research on social protest movements. Little concentrated attention has been given to analysis of the black church as it might have influenced civil rights militancy of blacks in the early 1960s. Scholars working within an assimilationist framework viewed black organizations as basically retarding the integration of black Americans into the larger society. The best-known spokesman for this position was E. Franklin Frazier, whose work on the black church has already been introduced. In a similar fashion, Kenneth B. Clark has commented that the black church is the "last and only sanctuary" from the larger society. While Clark writes that "the church as an institution has not yet found the formula for effecting change without alienating its strongest supporters," he nevertheless recognizes the potential of the black church. "Only in the most segregated of social institutions, the church, was [the Negro] able to exercise that degree of personal and racial freedom necessary for the initial stages of an effective campaign against racial injustices. The Negro church, therefore, cannot be understood primarily in traditional theological terms, but rather in terms of the religion of race. For the Negro, his church is his instrument of escape, his weapon of protest, his protective fortress behind which he plans his strategies of defiance, harassment, and at times, his frontal attacks against racial barriers."[1] Partly because of this special role of the black church, it remains the least desegregated institution for black membership. Yet Clark argues that the black church's rewards, like all other satisfactions deriving from segregation, are inferior. Only by rejecting the old, known comforts of such ghetto institutions can black people hope to qualify for the rewards of the open society.[2]

The only direct analysis of the relationship between religiosity and militancy was completed by Gary Marx using data collected in late 1964 as part of the University of California *Five-Year Study of Anti-Semitism in the United States*. The 1,119 black interviews were conducted in a general nonsouthern metropolitan sample, as well as in samples from Chicago, New York, Atlanta, and Birmingham.[3]

Marx published his findings on this analysis of the relationship between religiosity and militancy in 1967. He reported that there were denominational differences among blacks (for example, Baptists were less likely to be militant than Episcopalians) and that militancy had an inverse relationship with the subjective importance assigned to religion, with frequency of attendance at worship services, and with orthodoxy of belief.[4] He combined subjective importance, attendance, and orthodoxy into an overall measure of religiosity and then showed an inverse relationship between religiosity and militancy.[5] After commenting that "it is possible that the relationship observed is simply a consequence of the fact that both religiosity and militancy are related to some third factor," he introduced as single controls the following variables: education, age, region, sex, and denomination.[6] Tests for significance were not reported. He concluded that the relationship continued to exist even with the introduction of a single control.

Yet Marx notes that "even for the militants, a majority were scored either 'very religious' or 'somewhat religious' " and consequently "for many, a religious orientation and a concern with racial protest are not mutually exclusive."[7] A dual orientation of religion enables it to serve both as an opiate and as an inspiration of civil rights militancy. Marx concludes that otherworldly religiosity tends to inhibit civil rights militancy, while religiosity with temporal concern tends to inspire militancy.[8] Concerning the present state of black religion of an otherworldly cast: "Until such time as religion loosens its hold over these people or comes to embody to a greater extent the belief that man as well as God can bring about secular change, and focuses more on the here and now, religious involvement may be seen as an important factor working against the widespread radicalization of the Negro public."[9]

In the revised edition of *Protest and Prejudice*, Marx presents a reanalysis of the data for the religiosity-militancy relationship. Here he reports five variables concerned one way or another with religiosity—denomination, number of memberships in church organizations, attendance at worship services, subjective importance of religion, and orthodoxy of belief. He excludes the otherworldly-temporal religious concern variable.[10] From reading his chapter assessing the influences of religiosity on militancy, one gathers that religious involvement tends to act more as an opiate than an inspiration for civil rights militancy, since all of the variables are inversely correlated with militancy. Even the denominational variable gives the reader an impression that black religion acts as an opiate of militancy, since only blacks who are members of predominantly white denominations especially tend to be militant.[11] In sum, Marx's perspective is in the tradition of E. Franklin Frazier, that black religion impedes civil rights and the integration of the black into the mainstream of American society.

*Reanalysis of the Marx Data*

In *Protest and Prejudice* Marx presented (in a footnote) the effects upon militancy of an additional variable—organizational involvement in churches. "The study also made use of an additional measure of religious involvement, membership in church organizations. . . . among those belonging to none, one, two, or three or more church organizations, the percentage militant decreases from 28 percent to 23 percent to 15 percent to 8 percent, respectively. Thus, organizational involvement in churches serves to decrease militancy."[12] Because tests of significance are not reported for this and the other religious variables as they are related to militancy and because such factors as age and sex are controlled in only a singular fashion (as the second control is introduced, the first is withdrawn), the data were obtained for a reanalysis.

It has already been noted that the reader gains the overall impression that black religion generally serves as an opiate of civil rights militancy, since each of the variables presented by Marx serves to depress militancy. In addition, while Marx observes that religiosity acts as an opiate for blacks with an otherworldly religious concern, he then presents tables (militancy by subjective importance of religion, by religious orthodoxy, and by frequency of attendance at worship service) with members of sects excluded, giving the impression that even when the sectarianism factor is controlled, religiosity in general dampens civil rights militancy.[13] Yet it is recognized by various scholars that heterogeneity of belief exists within as well as among national denominations.[14] Indeed, the import of Demerath's *Social Class in American Protestantism* is that there is considerable variation in membership involvement in terms of churchlike and sectlike religiosity.[15] An effective control for sectarianism can hardly be introduced by merely excluding members of sects and cults from the analysis of the data, which was the technique employed by Marx.[16]

To summarize the difficulties in accepting Marx's analyses, first, the general finding that religiosity acts as an opiate of militancy may well be due to a strong, inverse relationship between sectarianism and militancy. Second, the relationship of religiosity and militancy may be spurious, caused by not simultaneously controlling for education, sex, and other correlates of militancy and religiosity.

Table 24 presents the eta and beta coefficients from five reanalyses of the data by Multiple Classification Analysis, using education, sex, and a religious predictor (in singular fashion: denomination, number of church organizational memberships, attendance, importance of religion, and orthodoxy) and beta coefficients from five reanalyses utilizing each of these religious predictors together with sex, education, income, and residential background of the respondent.[17]

The percentage militant for each of the categories of these religiosity variables is shown in Table 25. Here the effect of adding the two controls (education and sex) can be seen in a dramatic fashion. With education and sex controlled, there is a percentage difference of only 8.5 between Baptists and members of predominantly white denominations who are militant. The relationship between attendance and militancy is slightly curvilinear, with respondents who attend less than monthly but at least once a year being most militant; only respondents attending more than once a week exhibit

*Table 24*

Effects of Selected Predictors on Militancy
(Marx Data)

| Predictors | Eta Coefficient | Beta Coefficient[a] | Beta Coefficient[b] |
|---|---|---|---|
| Denomination | -.13 | -.08[c] | -.08[c] |
| Church memberships | -.07[d] | -.05[c] | -.04[c] |
| Attendance | -.10[d] | -.06[c] | -.05[c] |
| Importance of religion | -.20 | -.14 | -.13 |
| Orthodoxy of belief | -.20 | -.15 | -.14 |

NOTE: Militancy has been dichotomized into low (scores 0-5) and high (scores 6-8). Marx's assignment of scores was utilized here.
[a]Controlling on education and sex.
[b]Controlling on income, residential background, education, and sex.
[c]Not significant at the .05 level, using appropriate F test of significance. Unless indicated, all other coefficients are significant at the .01 level.
[d]Significant at the .05 level.

strikingly lower militancy. While diminished, the effects of subjective importance of religion and orthodoxy of belief remain significant.

The percentage difference in militancy of respondents belonging to no church organizations and respondents belonging to one or more organizations connected with a church is only 5.3. As can be seen from Table 24, the value for the beta coefficient is -.05, with controls for education and sex. A separate analysis using the number of nonchurch memberships (coded as none, one, two or more), education, and sex as predictors of militancy resulted in the eta coefficient for membership being +.11 (significant at the .01 level) and the beta coefficient being +.05 (not significant at the .05 level). Utilizing income and residential background as well, the beta coefficient for membership was +.03 (not significant at the .05 level). In sum, we can hardly say that membership in church organizations and membership in nonchurch organizations act in quite opposite directions; the effects of these two variables are minimal.

While the directions of all relationships reported in Table 24 are negative, only on two variables (importance of religion and ortho-

*Table 25*

## Percentage Militant by Selected Predictors
### (Marx Data)

| Predictor & Controls | Percentage Militant by Category | | | | |
|---|---|---|---|---|---|
| Denomination | Mostly white churches[a] | Catholic[b] | Methodist | Baptist | Sect and cult |
| None | 40.0 | 36.4 | 28.4 | 25.3 | 16.0 |
| Education, sex | 35.0 | 32.0 | 26.3 | 26.5 | 18.5 |
| (N) | (60) | (107) | (141) | (656) | (106) |

| Number of church organizational memberships | None | One or more |
|---|---|---|
| None | 28.3 | 20.8 |
| Education, sex | 27.9 | 22.6 |
| (N) | (844) | (250) |

| Attendance at worship services | Less than yearly | Less than monthly | Less than weekly | Once a week | More than once a week |
|---|---|---|---|---|---|
| None | 31.7 | 33.7 | 27.2 | 25.0 | 16.8 |
| Education, sex | 28.5 | 30.7 | 27.3 | 26.1 | 20.2 |
| (N) | (63) | (181) | (379) | (348) | (113) |

| Subjective importance of religion | Not at all | Not too | Fairly | Quite | Extremely |
|---|---|---|---|---|---|
| None | 61.5 | 52.6 | 43.6 | 31.7 | 21.7 |
| Education, sex | 50.3 | 46.7 | 39.3 | 29.7 | 23.1 |
| (N) | (13) | (19) | (101) | (205) | (752) |

| Orthodoxy of belief | Low 0 | 1 | 2 | 3 | 4 | 5 | High 6 |
|---|---|---|---|---|---|---|---|
| None | 53.3 | 43.4 | 39.0 | 23.4 | 23.0 | 24.6 | 20.3 |
| Education, sex | 45.6 | 39.6 | 35.6 | 21.2 | 23.5 | 25.8 | 22.9 |
| (N) | (45) | (53) | (118) | (137) | (235) | (171) | (330) |

[a]Includes Episcopalian, United Church of Christ, and Presbyterian.
[b]Following Marx, this category includes "None."

doxy of belief) are the effects significant. Both of these variables are, no doubt, related to an otherworldly religious spirit, and consequently the reader should not infer from Marx's writings that he has been able to demonstrate that religiosity in general means depressed militancy on the part of blacks. It seems safe to conclude, however, that an otherworldly religious orientation acts as an opiate of civil rights militancy. It is this topic, contrasting thisworldly and otherworldly religious orientations as related to militancy, to which we next turn.

### Measures of Orthodoxy and Sectarianism

In the introductory chapter it was observed that the church-sect typology implies a conservative orientation of the religious organization toward social issues since the church takes an accommodative role toward the secular society and since the sect generally encourages an otherworldly orientation on the part of its black members. Church and sect are ideal types of religious organizations, but the concepts have also been utilized in contrasting individual churchlike and sectlike orientations.[18] Demerath observes that church and sect differ on two axes, internal characteristics and the relationship with the external world.

> *Internally,* the church has a professional leadership, a relatively impersonal fellowship, and lax criteria for membership. It stresses the sacraments and ritualistic religion. In sharp contrast, the sect's leadership is charismatic and non-professional. . . . Further the sect's membership standards are stringent and include conversion and signs of salvation. . . .
> *Externally,* the church accommodates the secular order. Its posture is one of adaptive compromise, and this leads to organizational stability and a large following. . . . Again in contrast, the sect is either aloof or antagonistic toward the secular society.[19]

In the previous chapter evidence was presented that black Americans are more likely than white Americans to desire civil rights protest on the part of their ministers and churches. As noted earlier, Myrdal observed that "the Negro church fundamentally is an expression of the Negro community itself [and] if the church has been other-worldly in outlook and indulged in emotional ecstasy, it is primarily because the downtrodden common Negroes have craved religious escape from poverty and other tribulations." Myrdal concluded that "when the Negro community changes, the church also will change."[20] With the black community being receptive to civil rights protest, an accommodative spirit on the part of the church could embrace militancy. It is the view here that the black church has had a much more positive orientation toward militancy than this conclusion might imply, that the black church has meant community integration and strength and that it has fostered protest, as well as providing self-esteem for its members.[21]

A churchlike orientation should be positively related to militancy if the black church can serve as an institutional means of protest, as Clark and others imply. On the other hand, a sectlike orientation, which is often otherworldly in orientation, should be inversely related to militancy.

The developing of measures to ascertain churchlike and sectlike orientations is difficult, in part because the two variables have in common a "proreligious" attitude.[22] Churchlike members will often endorse many of the items found in a sectlike scale—that many of their best friends belong to their church, for example, and, even more likely, that church membership is of great help in many areas of their life. These items are from Demerath who divides six measures of religiosity into two contrasting indexes of religious commitment (with each index containing three items), which he labels indexes of churchlike and sectlike religiosity. Theoretically these two measures should be inversely related, but from Table 26 it can be seen instead that they are positively related, testifying to the presence of the "proreligious" variable. Whether this variable is an artificial construct produced in large part by response set in interviewing or is an effect caused by a mechanism that is not artificial, be it cognitive consistency or the influence of church participation itself, will not be the subject of extensive analysis here.

That participation in church life itself might well be a linking factor is suggested by the results of a reanalysis of the Lenski data. Lenski was interested in degree and type of involvement in the socioreligious group, and here he contrasted associational and com-

*Table 26*

## Percentage of Demerath's Respondents Exhibiting Sectlike Religiosity, by Churchlike Religiosity

| | *Churchlike Religiosity* | | | *.05 Two-Sided* |
|---|---|---|---|---|
| | *Low* | *High* | *Q* | *Confidence Limits* |
| Percentage exhibiting sectlike religiosity | 37.8 | 50.6 | +.26 | +.17 and +.34 |
| (N) | (912) | (1,183) | | |

SOURCE: This table is derived from frequencies reported in Demerath, *Social Class,* p. 81.

munal involvement, with the former including attendance at religious services as one of two items of the index. Lenski also laid great emphasis upon religious orientation, and in this context he compared respondents in terms of doctrinal orthodoxy and devotionalism. While Lenski reported negligible relationships between the two types of involvement and between the two religious orientations, he did not investigate relationships across these two types of variables (involvement and religious orientation). One might speculate that a possible linkage between the two types of variables might come through associational involvement, since church participation should affect both personal belief and ritual. Table 27 presents the percentage exhibiting high devotionalism (as measured by Lenski who dichotomized the variable) by attendance at services.[23]

As can be seen from this table, attendance and devotionalism were found to be strongly related. Attendance reflects to some degree public piety, while devotionalism consists more of a private piety, a turning to God in moments of decision and for comfort. The former is more instrumental, while the latter is more expressive; and, as Demerath notes, "Activities of the instrumental type are . . . more churchlike."[24] Expressive behavior is often interpreted as more sectlike than churchlike, while, conversely, instrumental behavior is viewed as more churchlike than sectlike. In America, expressive religious behavior is coupled with lower-class status, while instrumental religious behavior is more characteristic of the middle and

*Table 27*

**Percentage of Lenski's Respondents Exhibiting High Devotionalism, by Attendance at Religious Services**

| Attendance | Percentage Giving Devotional Response | Adjusted Percentage[a] | N | Coefficients Eta | Beta |
|---|---|---|---|---|---|
| Never | 17.5 | 21.4 | 57 | | |
| Few times a year | 14.8 | 18.8 | 88 | | |
| Once a month | 33.3 | 38.4 | 30 | | |
| Twice a month | 45.5 | 37.2 | 77 | | |
| Once a week or more | 54.5 | 53.8 | 220 | +.35 | +.30 |

NOTE: N=472; R=.52 (d.f.=23); all coefficients shown were significant at the .001 level.

[a]The following predictors were utilized in the analysis: sex, age, education of respondent, region of the U.S. where born, size of community where born, income, attendance, socio-religious group, and occupation of head.

upper classes. Yet in Table 27 we see the expressive and instrumental forms *positively* related.

The calculation of the value of Q coefficient for the Demerath churchlike and sectlike religiosity data and the reanalysis of the Lenski data serve to introduce us to the problem of the "pror_eligion" orientation which probably stems in part from religious participation. Marx's *religiosity index* consisted of summated responses for attendance, subjective importance of religion, and orthodoxy of belief. It has not been utilized in this reanalysis precisely because it is open to the problem under discussion, namely, proreligion.[25]

Finally, a comment on Marx's *orthodoxy index* is in order. It included summated responses to three items: belief in God, eternal life, and the devil. The last item clearly represents fundamentalism, a literalistic view of the Bible and evil. The first two items more represent Christian orthodoxy. To what degree the last item and proreligion carry the orthodoxy index is uncertain. In sum, Marx's index can be faulted on two accounts: first, it is concerned with religiosity in general (including proreligion) and second, it is perhaps more sectlike than churchlike.

Partly in order to assess more directly the impact of religiosity upon militancy, interviewing was conducted in the 1970-1971 academic year in Bowling Green, Kentucky, resulting in 405 completed black interviews out of 418 sampled respondents (a completion rate of 97 percent). A more complete description of the sample is found in Appendix A. Measures of orthodoxy, sectarianism, and churchlike and sectlike involvement were included in the study.

The orthodoxy scale as developed by Lenski was used. Lenski notes that the six questions used in the scale were designed only for classifying Christians and that they were labeled "orthodox" only if they gave assertion to *all* six questions.[26] This, then, was a strict definition of orthodoxy. Concerning socioreligious group differences, Lenski reports that of the Catholic respondents 62 percent "took an orthodox stance on all items, compared with only 38 per cent of the Negro Protestants and 32 per cent of the white Protestants."[27] Of the black respondents from the Bowling Green data, 58.1 percent were scored as orthodox (with a total N of 394, deleting respondents who could not be classified because of nonresponses to orthodoxy items), indicating that blacks of Bowling Green are somewhat more orthodox than blacks of Detroit.[28] In contrasting the Bowling Green and Detroit respondents, it must be remembered that Bowling Green is located in the border South, an area which is more conservative in terms of religious ideology; in addition, the cities are not the same in size, with Bowling Green having a 1970 total population of 36,253.[29] This difference, then, is not surprising.

Over 90 percent of the Bowling Green respondents positively endorsed each of the orthodoxy items except for the item concerning life after death (77.0 percent endorsement) and the related item concerning punishment or reward in the next life (63.7 percent); this two-part item, then, carries much of the weight of the orthodoxy scale.[30] This item concerning punishment or reward by God in the next life is colored by a strong tinge of sectarianism, but with this exception the index appears to measure orthodoxy.

A measurement of sectarianism in terms of religious ideology presents us with a more difficult problem. Here Earl D. C. Brewer gives us a lead when he compares Old and New Testament views of God in his analysis of southern Appalachian religion. The former

*Table 28*

Percentage Sectarian by Orthodoxy

| | Orthodoxy | | | .05 One-Sided |
| --- | --- | --- | --- | --- |
| | Heterodox | Orthodox | Q | Confidence Limits |
| Percentage sectarian | 46.2 | 37.7 | -.17 | -.00 and -.34 |
| (N) | (143) | (223) | | |

view includes God as "righteous judge of all men" while the latter pictures God more as "loving Heavenly Father."[31] Two sectarian items from a six-item scale of religious conservatism were used, along with two other items which are colored with orthodoxy; the resulting four items were shown to have face-validity and internal reliability.[32]

The two sectarianism items concerning testifying and God as sending misfortune were the harshest items of a six-item scale for religious ideology. The scale was developed for white southern Appalachian Presbyterians and was clearly shown to have face-validity and predictive validity and high inter-item consistency among the responses for the population under study.[33] For the Bowling Green black responses, the six-item scale was not unidimensional, since the two sectarian items were not always positively (and significantly) related to the other four items.[34] For the black responses, the sectarianism scale was judged to be acceptable in terms of both validity and internal reliability.[35]

While 58.1 percent of the 394 respondents who could be categorized on orthodoxy were orthodox rather than heterodox, 40.9 percent of the 374 respondents who could be categorized on sectarianism were high rather than low on sectarianism. The relationship between these two variables can be seen in Table 28. That these two variables measure opposite orientations, namely, churchlike and sectlike religious ideologies, is given credibility since the relationship is inverse, even though only approaching significance, doubtless a result partly of small sample size and partly of the hidden effects of a proreligion variable which would tend to make the relationship positive rather than inverse. In other words, we have been quite successful in finding two measures of churchlike and sectlike orientations which are inverse, as they should be in terms of church-sect theory. This was accomplished by turning to religious ideology rather than religious organizational involvement; and for whites the relationship might well be positive rather than inverse, suggesting that sectarianism here is a residual religious variable for blacks only (later in this chapter we will examine this more carefully by relating these two variables to education). It is these two measures of orthodoxy and sectarianism that we will employ in analyzing the relationship between religiosity and militancy, but before proceeding to a description of the militancy scale and the analysis of the relationship, let us digress by introducing two additional churchlike and sectlike measures which are concerned, instead, with organizational involvement and which we will later add to orthodoxy and sectarianism for a summated index.

### Measures of Churchlike and Sectlike Involvement

Concentrating upon the Lutheran data of the Effective City Church study begun in 1957 by the National Council of Churches of Christ in the U.S.A., Demerath, as already noted, developed two indexes of church participation. He used six measures of religiosity to develop the two indexes. "Three reflect a churchlike commitment: Sunday service attendance, parish activities, and outside organizations. Three connote a sectlike involvement: the number of close friends in the congregation, religious aid, and disapproval of the minister's participation in community affairs and controversy."[36]

Similar but not identical questions were included in the Bowling Green interview schedule and from these, two measures of involvement together with two measures to test predictive validity were developed. Three churchlike items having to do with membership and/or participation in nonchurch organizations included:

> To how many organizations, societies, or clubs do you belong?
> On the average, how often do you attend meetings of these organizations—regularly, occasionally, rarely, or never?
> Have you ever been an officer in these organizations?[37]

*Table 29*

Percentage High in Churchlike Involvement,
by Levels of Intrinsic Church Involvement

| | *Levels of Intrinsic Church Involvement* | | | | | *Chi-* | | |
|---|---|---|---|---|---|---|---|---|
| | *0* | *1* | *2* | *3* | *Gamma* | *Square* | *d.f.* | *P* |
| Percentage with churchlike involvement[a] | 13.5 | 24.3 | 54.5 | 82.0 | +.75 | 127.51 | 3 | .001 |
| (N) | (104) | (74) | (99) | (128) | | | | |

[a]Churchlike involvement was dichotomized into low (score 0) and high (scores 1-2). Shown are percent high.

Two churchlike items having to do with membership and/or participation in church organizations included:

Do you take part in any of the activities or organizations of your church other than attending services?
How often have you done these things in the past year?[38]

An additional measure was constructed to permit a testing of the validity of the measure just introduced.[39] This additional measure was designed to reflect intrinsic enjoyment and a feeling of full participation in organizational involvement.[40]

Table 29 presents the relationship between this additional measure of churchlike involvement, one that is designed to measure a feeling of enjoyment in participation as well as a feeling of complete participation, and the summated churchlike involvement index. The churchlike involvement index can be said to have predictive validity, based on the data presented in Table 29.

For the sectlike involvement index one measure of communalism and three items on saliency were utilized. The communalism measure was:

Think of your five closest friends. How many of them are members of your local congregation?[41]

*Table 30*

Percentage High in Sectlike Behavior, by Belief the
Church Should Not Be Involved in Political Matters

|  | *Levels of Belief Disfavoring Political Involvement* | | | | | *Chi-* | | |
| --- | --- | --- | --- | --- | --- | --- | --- | --- |
|  | *0* | *1* | *2* | *3* | *Gamma* | *Square* | *d.f.* | *P* |
| Percentage with sectlike involvement[a] | 17.9 | 24.0 | 40.4 | 49.5 | +.39 | 25.72 | 3 | .001 |
| (N) | (67) | (129) | (114) | (95) | | | | |

[a]Sectlike involvement was dichotomized into low (scores 0-2) and high (scores 3-4). Shown are percent high.

The three items on saliency were:

How much interest do you have in religion? Would you say much, some, little, or none?

All things considered, do you think you are more interested, about as interested, or less interested in religion than you were five or ten years ago?

Religion is especially important to me because it answers many questions about the meaning of life—agree, unsure, disagree.[42]

Demerath held that the sectarian is averse to participation by the minister in community affairs and controversial subjects.[43] A second measure of sectlike involvement was developed utilizing the sectarian respondent's desire for noninvolvement on the part of the church.[44] This additional measure was designed for the purpose of testing the predictive validity of the sectlike involvement index.[45]

Table 30 presents the relationship between this additional measure of sectlike orientation (here, the preference of religious over political goals) and the sectlike involvement index. The sectlike index can be said to have predictive validity, based on the data presented in Table 30.

From an examination of the inter-item correlations for the two

*Table 31*

## Percentage High in Churchlike Involvement
## by Orthodoxy of Religious Ideology

| | Orthodoxy[a] | | | .05 Two-Sided |
|---|---|---|---|---|
| | Heterodox | Orthodox | Q | Confidence Limits |
| Percentage high in churchlike involvement | 38.1 | 54.1 | +.32 | +.14 and +.50 |
| (N) | (176) | (229) | | |

[a]No responses on the orthodoxy index are counted here as heterodox. With no responses deleted, the percentages are 38.8 (N=165) and 54.1 (N=229) and Q=+.30, with .05 two-sided confidence limits of +.12 and +.49.

measures (churchlike and sectlike involvement) and from cross-tabulations with the two additional measures, we can place confidence in the reliability and validity of the two indexes. The value of Q for the interrelationship between these two measures of involvement is +.58, reminding us that while these measures are concerned with theoretically opposite orientations, that is, churchlike and sectlike involvement, they have in common an involvement in the religious organization and hence are positively related.

It might be expected that orthodoxy and churchlike involvement should be positively associated. The relationship can be seen from Table 31. The value of Q is +.32 and is significant at the .05 level.

The relationship between sectarianism and sectlike involvement theoretically would be positive in direction, but here a negligible degree of association was expected because of the positive relationship between churchlike and sectlike involvement. The data are summarized in Table 32. A low positive association was found.

### A Measure of Civil Rights Militancy

Before employing these measures of religiosity, it will be necessary to introduce a measure of civil rights militancy. Eight items were employed for scale analysis.[46] An examination of the content of the items and of internal reliability and unidimensionality leaves little

*Table 32*

### Percentage High in Sectlike Involvement
### by Sectarianism of Religious Ideology

|  | *Sectarianism*[a] | | | *.05 Two-Sided* |
|---|---|---|---|---|
|  | *Low* | *High* | *Q* | *Confidence Limits* |
| Percentage high in sectlike involvement | 29.8 | 39.9 | +.22 | +.02 and +.42 |
| (N) | (252) | (153) | | |

[a]"No responses" on the sectarianism index are counted as low in sectarianism. With "no responses" deleted, however, the percentages are 32.1 (N=221) and 39.9 (N=153) and Q=+.17, with .05 one-sided confidence limits of −.00 and +.34.

doubt that strong confidence can be placed in the scale's validity and reliability.[47] One must recognize, of course, that the scale is bound by its administration at a particular time—what is militant at one point may at a later date reflect a more passive orientation. While an examination of skewness and kurtosis also indicated the acceptability of the scale and while the scale had unidimensionality and thus it might be assumed that the scale scores could be treated as interval data without undue bias, nevertheless, the scale scores were dichotomized, with scores of 5 through 8 treated as high (or with a value of 1). Thus it was possible to assign most respondents to either the low or the high categories on the basis of the responses they actually made; in cases of doubt, due to missing data, respondents' scores were deleted.[48] Consequently, Multiple Classification Analysis can be nicely employed, with militancy as a dichotomized variable, giving readable percentages of militancy rather than mean scores.

*Militancy by Proreligion and by*
*Sectlike Religiosity Style*

Earlier, two measures of religious ideology (orthodoxy and sectarianism) and two measures of religious involvement (churchlike and sectlike) were presented. Here these scores (in dichotomized form)

## Table 33

### Effects of Education, Sex, and Proreligion on Militancy

| Predictors | Eta Coefficient | Beta Coefficient |
|---|---|---|
| Education | +.33 | +.31 |
| Sex | −.16 | −.13 |
| Proreligion | −.11[a] | −.09[a] |

NOTE: N=382; R=.338 (d.f.=9).

[a]Not significant at the .05 level, using appropriate F test of significance. Unless indicated, all other coefficients are significant at the .01 level.

have been summed in two forms—first, by adding all positive scores across the four measures for a proreligious variable and, second, by adding all sectarian scores (reversing the direction of the orthodoxy and churchlike involvement measures) across the four measures for a sectlike religiosity style variable.

The relationship between proreligion (or a summated religiosity variable) and militancy should be somewhat curvilinear, with the highest percentage scoring militant toward the low end of the variable. At the same time, it would be expected that the variable of proreligion should not be significantly related to militancy. The results of the analysis are shown in Tables 33 and 34, which present the values for the eta and beta coefficients, using proreligion, education, and sex as predictor variables. The percentages militant by proreligion are shown in Table 34. Education and sex are the two major variables associated with both religiosity and with civil rights militancy; and, as in the reanalysis of the Marx data, these are the two major variables employed as controls.[49] The data are from Bowling Green, Kentucky. There was a more or less inverse relationship between proreligion and militancy, and this relationship was not significant at the .05 level either with or without control for education and sex. In sum, religiosity per se is not related to militancy.

Tables 35 and 36 present the values for eta and beta coefficients, using sectlike involvement, education, and sex as predictor variables, and percentages militant by sectlike religiosity style. Here there was a definite inverse relationship between sectlike style and militancy,

Table 34

## Percentage Militant by Proreligion

| Proreligion Score | | N | Percentage in Category | Percentage Militant | Adjusted Percentage[a] |
|---|---|---|---|---|---|
| Low | 0 | 56 | 14.7 | 41.1 | 38.0 |
| | 1 | 116 | 30.4 | 45.7 | 44.6 |
| | 2 | 100 | 26.2 | 42.0 | 43.8 |
| | 3 | 88 | 23.0 | 36.4 | 35.5 |
| High | 4 | 22 | 5.8 | 22.7 | 32.1 |

[a]Adjusting for the effects of education and sex.

*Table 35*

## Effects of Education, Sex, and Sectlike Style on Militancy

| Predictors | Eta Coefficient | Beta Coefficient |
|---|---|---|
| Education | +.33 | +.29 |
| Sex | −.16 | −.12 |
| Sectlike style[a] | −.22 | −.17 |

NOTE: N=382; R=.366 (d.f.=9).
[a]All coefficients are significant at the .01 level, except the beta coefficient for sectlike religiosity style which is significant at the .05 level.

*Table 36*

## Percentage Militant by Sectlike Religiosity Style

| Score for Sectlike Religiosity Style | | N | Percentage in Category | Percentage Militant | Adjusted Percentage[a] |
|---|---|---|---|---|---|
| Low | 0 | 35 | 9.2 | 62.9 | 60.0 |
| | 1 | 139 | 36.4 | 48.2 | 45.4 |
| | 2 | 136 | 35.6 | 34.6 | 36.1 |
| | 3 | 65 | 17.0 | 27.7 | 30.8 |
| High | 4 | 7 | 1.8 | 14.3 | 27.2 |

[a]Adjusting for the effects of education and sex.

### Table 37

### Effects of Education, Sex, and Orthodoxy on Militancy

| Predictors | Eta Coefficient | Beta Coefficient |
|---|---|---|
| Education | +.35 | +.33 |
| Sex | -.18 | -.16 |
| Orthodoxy | +.08[a] | +.10[b] |

NOTE: N=373; R=.374 (d.f.=6).
[a]Not significant at the .05 level, using appropriate F test of significance. Unless indicated, all other coefficients are significant at the .01 level.
[b]Significant at the .05 level.

as was expected. While 40.6 percent of the respondents were militant, at the lowest end of the sectlike style 60.0 percent were militant, compared to 27.2 percent at the highest end of the sectlike style variable.[50]

### Orthodoxy, Sectarianism, and Militancy

It has been observed that militancy is located at the churchlike end of the religiosity style variable. At this point it would seem judicious to take the two major indexes, those measuring orthodoxy and sectarianism, and to analyze the effects of these two variables on militancy, controlling again on education and sex. Table 37 reports the eta and beta coefficients using education, sex, and orthodoxy as predictors; Table 38 reports the percentage militant by heterodoxy and orthodoxy. The effects of education, sex, and sectarianism are shown in Tables 39 and 40, with the Table 39 indicating eta and beta coefficients and Table 40 summarizing the effect of sectarianism on militancy by percentage. As can be seen from these tables, orthodoxy and sectarianism act in opposite ways on militancy, with orthodoxy and militancy positively related and sectarianism and militancy inversely related. All beta coefficients are significant at least at the .05 level of probability. As indicated earlier, orthodoxy is related to churchlike involvement in religious organizations while sectarianism, as measured, is probably only nominally related to

### Table 38

### Percentage Militant by Orthodoxy

| Orthodoxy | N | Percentage in Category | Percentage Militant | Adjusted Percentage[a] |
|---|---|---|---|---|
| Heterodox | 152 | 40.8 | 35.5 | 34.3 |
| Orthodox | 221 | 59.2 | 43.9 | 44.8 |

[a] Adjusting for the effects of education and sex.

### Table 39

### Effects of Education, Sex, and Sectarianism on Militancy

| Predictors | Eta Coefficient[a] | Beta Coefficient[a] |
|---|---|---|
| Education | +.34 | +.31 |
| Sex | −.17 | −.13 |
| Sectarianism | −.16 | −.10[b] |

NOTE: N=354; R=.362 (d.f.=6).
[a] Unless indicated, all coefficients are significant at the .01 level.
[b] Significant at the .05 level.

### Table 40

### Percentage Militant by Sectarianism

| Level of Sectarianism | N | Percentage in Category | Percentage Militant | Adjusted Percentage[a] |
|---|---|---|---|---|
| Low | 212 | 59.9 | 46.7 | 44.4 |
| High | 142 | 40.1 | 31.0 | 34.8 |

[a] Adjusting for the effects of education and sex.

## Table 41

### Percentage Sectarian by Level of Education

|  | Grade 9 or Less | Grades 10-11 | High School Diploma | Some College or More |
|---|---|---|---|---|
| Percentage sectarian[a] | 58.0 | 42.3 | 39.0 | 30.0 |
| (N) | (81) | (104) | (59) | (130) |

NOTE: Gamma= −.31 Chi-square=16.39 d.f.=3 P<.001.

[a]Of the 374 respondents who could be classified, 40.9 percent were sectarian.

sectlike involvement in religious organizations. The influence of involvement in the religious organization, then, may well favor the development of militancy; but this topic is left for further research.

Sectarian religious ideology in many ways is a residual variable, since it is more or less uncorrelated with participation in the religious organization. The movement of many blacks to the cities and to the North has been one factor in the great degree of acculturation which has taken place, in religious style as well as in other areas of life. It has especially meant diminished emphasis on emotionalism and otherworldliness in religion. Another contributing factor to acculturation is education. Using the Bowling Green black data, we found an examination of the relationship between age and level of education instructive at this point: the substantial inverse relationship between these two variables (with gamma = −.55, significant at the .001 level) signifies that the younger black population has a higher educational level.

Rising educational levels should have an effect on sectarianism, with the significance of this residual variable decreasing. On the other hand, a low negative association or none at all might be expected for the relationship between education and orthodoxy. Tables 41 and 42 indicate the percentages sectarian and orthodox by educational levels. As can be seen from Table 41, there is a moderate inverse relationship between education and sectarianism, and this relationship, coupled with the rising educational level in the black community, augurs the eventual disappearance of this residual variable. From Table 42, however, it can be said that the future does not

**Orthodoxy and Sectarianism   121**

Table 42

## Percentage Orthodox by Level of Education

|  | Grade 9 or Less | Grades 10-11 | High School Diploma | Some College or More |
|---|---|---|---|---|
| Percentage orthodox[a] | 60.5 | 61.6 | 56.7 | 54.4 |
| (N) | (86) | (112) | (60) | (136) |

NOTE: Gamma= −.09 Chi-square=1.57 d.f.=3 P>.05.

[a]Of the 394 respondents who could be classified, 58.1 percent were orthodox.

seem to hold the same end for orthodoxy, as there is at most a negligible negative association between education and orthodoxy. From the vantage point of education, orthodoxy cannot be said to be residual; indeed, as noted earlier, orthodoxy was positively correlated with involvement in the religious organization.

### Summary

In this chapter a direct examination of the relationship between religiosity and militancy has been reported. From a secondary analysis of the Gary Marx data, it has been shown that of the dimensions of religiosity only subjective importance of religion and orthodoxy of belief are inversely related to militancy and it has been suggested that these relationships exist because of the effects of sectarianism, which are basically uncontrolled by Marx in his analysis. From reading Marx, however, the reader gains the impression that religiosity in general is inversely related to militancy.

A sectlike religiosity style index was developed and shown to be inversely related to militancy. Using this variable plus an index of orthodoxy, a separate proreligion index was summated; and the effects of this variable on militancy were reported. The relationship, which was slightly curvilinear (and more or less inverse), was not significant at the .05 level of probability.

Finally two components of the religiosity style—orthodoxy and sectarianism—were separately related to militancy, with the former having a positive and the latter a negative association with militancy.

In sum, a churchlike orientation inspires militancy, while a sectlike orientation acts as an opiate for militancy. Rising educational levels are coupled with a decrease in sectarianism but not in orthodoxy, signifying that Marx's comment about the necessity for a loss of the hold of religion over black people reflects both a viewpoint in the tradition of Frazier (i.e., that religion bars the assimilation of black people) and a belief that sectarianism is not rapidly disappearing among these Americans. In both cases Marx appears to be wrong: not all religion is inversely related to militancy, and sectarianism would appear to be waning as black educational levels rise.

# 7:

## Summary and Implications

The overall concern of this study has been with assessing black religion as acting as an opiate or an inspiration for civil rights militancy. Such an evaluation required a comparison of black and white Americans on various dimensions of religiosity as well as on attitudes toward social change in race relations. A direct analysis of the relationship between religious ideology and militancy served to throw greater light on the basic question. This final chapter, besides briefly summarizing the main findings, will consider the relationship between minority status (or consciousness of being a member of an ethnic or minority group) and the greater development of ethnic institutions, particularly the church. Implications of the findings in terms of the viability of the black church will be drawn.

*Summary*

The role of the religious institution in the development of larger community integration (i.e., integration within the ethnic community) and in the politicization of the ethnic members in terms of militancy has received short shrift from social scientists. Metzger has suggested that a sociological bias favoring the consensus model (which would have assimilation as a goal) has acted as a blinder, preventing description and analysis of civil rights and black power movements.[1] An additional factor hindering research on the black church has been a general stereotype of black religiosity as sectarian and thus as not concerned with social problems. The assimilationist view held by E. Franklin Frazier, with a concomitant perspective of the black chruch as anti-intellectual and as providing a refuge for the masses and hindering their full integration into American society, was generally accepted by most scholars as conclusive. Yet the black church was one of the several basic institutions of the black community and was acknowledged to be important in the life of black people.

A view of the black church as an ethnic institution with a life cycle would have religion offering compensation for temporal ills in the early stage of the ethnic community, whetting political appetites and building ethnic community solidarity at an intermediate stage, and waning as assimilation occurs at a final stage. Such a life cycle perspective, however, assumes a unilinear view of change, and of course social change does not always occur in this fashion. Ethnicity can increase and be revived as well as diminish.[2] With the realization by blacks that the hopes of the period of the mid-1960s, when assimilation appeared to be the dominant theme, were not to be achieved, and with increasing feelings of unity or consciousness of ethnicity or of minority status, the black church, along with other ethnic institutions, again started coming into its own, as shown by such evidence as increased attendance at worship services. The black church, as one of the institutions central to the black community, would function to provide a base for social solidarity not only for its members but for all of the individuals caught up in its social web, as Breton's analysis of institutional completeness shows.[3]

### The Three Models: Keeping the
### Faith in the Sixties

As we have already suggested, among social scientists who have seriously examined the black church since the great migration (beginning around World War I), three basic models can be discerned. The first model we termed assimilationist, or the isolation-integration model; numbered among its adherents are E. Franklin Frazier, Kenneth B. Clark, and Gary T. Marx. The second or compensatory model is to some degree a transitional model and is most prominently represented in the work of St. Clair Drake, Horace Cayton, and Gunnar Myrdal. The third model has been termed the ethnic community model and is an essentially positive view which is embraced by, among others, Benjamin Mays, Joseph Nicholson, and such theoreticians of black power and the church as Gayraud Wilmore and James Cone. Because of the leadership potential within this model—in which the church is viewed as providing community solidarity and the ministers increasingly are expected to be "race men"—it can also be termed the ethnic community-prophetic model. It is our thesis, based on an analysis of Gallup poll data on church attendance (to appear in the next section of this chapter) and of attitudes toward the church speaking out on social issues and toward ministerial involvement in political protest, that the church may well be moving into a realization of the ethnic community-prophetic model currently supported by black power elements within the church. This trend is highlighted by comparisons with the white church which appears instead to be drifting farther away from any kind of challenging or activist role.

Dr. Gayraud Wilmore (now the Martin Luther King, Jr., Professor of Social Ethics at Boston University) was chairman of the Division of Church and Race, Board of National Missions, of the United Presbyterian Church in the U.S.A. when he called for a revolution in black and white church relations. From his perch in the bureaucracy of a major white Protestant denomination, Wilmore was acutely aware of the dilemma of black congregations in white denominations and, ultimately, in white society. The idea of an integrated church in an integrated society seemed, for the moment at least, morally bankrupt. Wilmore searingly denounced the moral corruption of racist American churches and the "one-way street" that whites assumed to be integration, where "everything black was subordinate and inferior and would have to be given up for everything white."[4] (Wilmore's recognition of the agonizing identity crisis facing the "whitenized" black church of the white denomination was not unusual. Clifton F. Brown has noted the tendency of the black members of "white" churches to embrace militancy more wholeheartedly than many members of the traditional black churches.[5] Still, Charles Hamilton's study of the black preacher shows that this is not always true. The West Indian Episcopalian congregation of Father Wooden, on New Rochelle, which had little sympathy for its minister's civil rights activities, is a striking example.[6]) Wilmore saw a prophetic future for these churches if they could manage to "recover their own self-respect by demythologizing the white cultural bag through which the faith was transmitted to them and in which they have curled themselves up so comfortably." If the church can so liberate itself through an immersion in black culture and the ideology of black power, Wilmore argued, these black churches "may be able to illuminate a theme from the left wing of the Protestant Reformation that the American experience has increasingly made opaque. Namely, that while the church is not permitted to create its own culture alongside the secular, it does stand in a dialectical relationship to culture—more often in opposition than accommodation—its most severe critic and reformer rather than its champion and celebrant."[7]

Wilmore was willing to look beyond an ethnocentric interlude to a new ecumenical Christianity. James H. Cone, writing in 1969, while admitting that the black church's heritage of suffering and obedience gives it a decided advantage over its white counterpart in carrying out a radical Christianity, is more concerned about structuring the black church into a truly living force in the black community. While he feels that the post-Civil War black church became much the same spiritual void as the white church, a few ministers, and he counts Martin Luther King, Jr., as one of these, made some congregations exceptions. He even suggests that "black power advocates are men who were inspired by his zeal for freedom, and black power is their attempt to make his dream a reality."[8] While Cone rejects the compensatory function of the church as a reason for its existence, he calls for a revolutionary church which will actively embrace its own. "It is time for the black churches to change their style and join the suffering of the black masses, proclaiming the gospel of the black Christ. Whether they will do this is not clear now. What is clear is that they are poised at the moment of irrevocable decision, between costly obedience and confirmed apostasy."[9]

The relative newness of the black power revolt in the church is, no doubt, in some degree responsible for the scarcity of systematic attempts to see if reality is catching up to the rhetoric of the movement. Analysis of the role of ethnicity in politics has been offered as a possible approach in assessing the extent to which the black community may be moving toward a possible reestablishment of the church in its ethnic community role, thus perhaps laying the

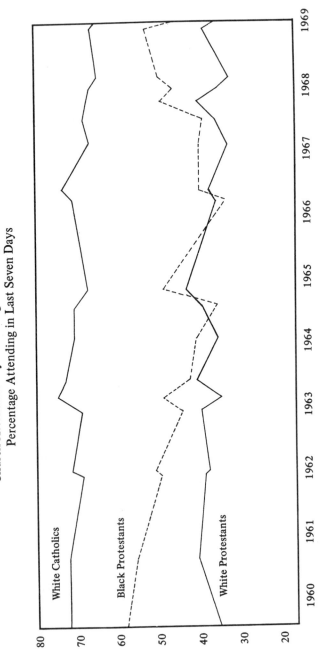

*Figure 1*

Church Attendance by Socioreligious Group and Date:
Percentage Attending in Last Seven Days

foundation for a more prophetic role for it in the future. While, as Robert Lane has observed, the early religious orientation of immigrant and black groups reduced political interest and activity partly because "religion offered an otherworldly solace for temporal ills," at a later date, the church can serve to whet the political appetite by increasing the social interaction of members as well as their perception of self-interest in political matters.[10] Lane also cites studies of the political activity of upwardly mobile individuals of ethnic background to suggest that "assimilation tends to depoliticize groups when it breaks up the homogeneity of ethnic associational life."[11]

### Ethnic Community and Attendance

Analysis of Gallup poll data over time might indicate whether the black community was indeed becoming increasingly politicized and what was happening during the same period to attitudes toward and participation in the church. The findings concerning attitude toward clergy protesting and the church speaking out on social and political issues have already been introduced: increasingly blacks desired a militant role on the part of the church, while whites increasingly desired a more passive outlook. It remains to present figures on church attendance and to examine more closely the possible relationship between attendance and the realization that assimilation cannot be a workable model.

The percentages (shown in Table 43) of white Catholic, black Protestant, and white Protestant respondents in 19 separate Gallup surveys spanning the period from 1960 to mid-1969 who reported attending church in the last seven days are plotted in Figure 1.[12] The black Protestant curve shows a steady decline in church attendance throughout the nonviolent, King-dominated period of the revolution when goals were sharply focused on integration. The black graph actually dips below the white Protestant graph in 1965 and 1966, a period characterized as uncertain, marked by the disintegration of the civil rights movement, the formulation of the black power position, and a justification of black violence. It is likely that the drop cannot be attributed to depressed attendance on the part of younger blacks participating in other activities linked with protest because, as we saw earlier in this study, attendance

Table 43

Percentage Attending Religious Services in the Last Seven Days
by Socioreligious Group and Date of Survey

| Date | Socioreligious Group | Percentage Attending | N | Difference of Proportions, Black and White Protestants, P |
|------|----------------------|----------------------|---|-----------------------------------------------------------|
| February 1960 | White Catholics | 72.5 | 819 | |
| | Black Protestants | 58.6 | 314 | |
| | White Protestants | 35.2 | 1,490 | <.001 |
| March 1961 | White Catholics | 72.5 | 723 | |
| | Black Protestants | 55.5 | 344 | |
| | White Protestants | 41.8 | 2,166 | <.001 |
| May 1962 | White Catholics | 69.2 | 816 | |
| | Black Protestants | 49.7 | 372 | |
| | White Protestants | 38.8 | 2,187 | <.001 |
| June 1962 | White Catholics | 72.1 | 767 | |
| | Black Protestants | 51.9 | 270 | |
| | White Protestants | 37.9 | 2,037 | <.001 |
| May 1963 | White Catholics | 69.5 | 773 | |
| | Black Protestants | 44.6 | 442 | |
| | White Protestants | 39.7 | 2,505 | <.05 |
| August 1963 | White Catholics | 75.0 | 811 | |
| | Black Protestants | 48.1 | 387 | |
| | White Protestants | 35.0 | 2,052 | <.001 |
| December 1963 | White Catholics | 72.8 | 931 | |
| | Black Protestants | 42.5 | 529 | |
| | White Protestants | 41.0 | 2,571 | >.05 |
| July 1964 | White Catholics | 71.7 | 658 | |
| | Black Protestants | 41.3 | 358 | |
| | White Protestants | 36.0 | 2,164 | >.05 |
| February 1965 | White Catholics | 71.4 | 297 | |
| | Black Protestants | 36.3 | 124 | |
| | White Protestants | 39.4 | 1,021 | >.05 |

| Date | Socioreligious Group | Percentage Attending | N | Difference of Proportions, Black and White Protestants, P |
|------|---------------------|---------------------|---|---------------------------------------------------------|
| April 1965 | White Catholics | 67.6 | 728 | |
| | Black Protestants | 48.7 | 337 | |
| | White Protestants | 43.0 | 2,082 | $<.05$ |
| September 1966 | White Catholics | 71.7 | 381 | |
| | Black Protestants | 33.9 | 112 | |
| | White Protestants | 36.2 | 908 | $>.05$ |
| December 1966 | White Catholics | 73.5 | 317 | |
| | Black Protestants | 40.0 | 125 | |
| | White Protestants | 37.6 | 892 | $>.05$ |
| August 1967 | White Catholics | 67.0 | 821 | |
| | Black Protestants | 40.2 | 246 | |
| | White Protestants | 33.6 | 2,166 | $<.05$ |
| January 1968 | White Catholics | 68.4 | 339 | |
| | Black Protestants | 39.5 | 86 | |
| | White Protestants | 36.4 | 937 | $>.05$ |
| April 1968 | White Catholics | 67.8 | 335 | |
| | Black Protestants | 48.6 | 74 | |
| | White Protestants | 40.2 | 929 | $>.05$ |
| June 1968 | White Catholics | 66.6 | 341 | |
| | Black Protestants | 46.2 | 104 | |
| | White Protestants | 35.3 | 944 | $<.05$ |
| August 1968 | White Catholics | 65.0 | 394 | |
| | Black Protestants | 49.1 | 112 | |
| | White Protestants | 33.4 | 893 | $<.01$ |
| Early May 1969 | White Catholics | 66.2 | 397 | |
| | Black Protestants | 52.8 | 108 | |
| | White Protestants | 38.6 | 871 | $<.01$ |
| Late May 1969 | White Catholics | 65.0 | 374 | |
| | Black Protestants | 46.8 | 94 | |
| | White Protestants | 36.5 | 891 | $<.05$ |

figures are kept high primarily by older blacks. By 1967 and 1968, with the effective abandonment of the earlier approach to civil rights, the black graph begins a sharp upward climb which continued into mid-1969. The Gallup data, then, may indicate that as the prospect of imminent assimilation faded, blacks returned to a strengthening of their ethnic associational life.

From an analysis of data collected in 1967-1968 in Indianapolis, Olsen reported that black respondents who identified themselves as members of an ethnic minority scored higher than nonidentifiers on the various measures of participation. For example, identifiers scored higher on church participation (but significance levels were not reported; probably the differences were nonsignificant, in part because of small sample size).[13]

A set of data collected in 1963-1964 for the *Public Images of Mental Health Services Study* included responses to a question concerning religious attendance in the past seven days as well as minority self-identification. The responses from the 304 black respondents (of a total of 2,118, all residents of New York City) were reanalyzed here.[14] The data for the *Public Images of Mental Health Services Study* were collected in a "multi-stage, probability area sample of housing units, with all persons 20 years of age and over in each housing unit to be interviewed, designed to yield a self-weighting sample of adults." It is noted that "this sample is representative of the five million adults living in New York City, with each borough represented in proportion to its adult population."[15] The sample design is described more fully in the complete report and comparisons are made between characteristics of interviewees and New York City 1960 census data.[16]

In the secondary analysis Multiple Classification Analysis was employed, with age, education, minority identification, and sex used as predictors. The eta and beta coefficients can be seen in Table 44. Of the 180 respondents who stated they did not feel they were members of a minority group, 23.3 percent (23.8 percent adjusting for the effects of the other predictors) reported attending services within the last seven days, compared to 38.3 percent (37.7 percent adjusted) of those who did so identify themselves. Not only were black identifiers more likely to attend by 1967-1968 (the time of the Olsen study), but in the earlier period, one with assimilationist

## Table 44

### Effects of Age, Education, Sex, and Minority Group Self-Identification on Attendance at Worship Services in the Past Week (New York City 1963-1964 Data, Blacks Only)

| Predictors[b] | Eta Coefficient | Beta Coefficient |
|---|---|---|
| Age | +.12[a] | +.11[a] |
| Education | +.15[a] | +.13[a] |
| Sex | -.16 | -.20 |
| Minority status | +.16 | +.15 |

NOTE: N=304; R=.251 (d.f.=9).

[a]Not significant at the .05 level, using appropriate F test of significance. Unless indicated, all other coefficients are significant at the .01 level.

[b]Age was coded 29 and under, 30-39, 40-49, and 50 and over; education was coded less than high school, some high school, high school diploma, and some college or more; sex was coded female and male; and minority status was coded no and yes.

goals, if anything they were even more likely than nonidentifiers to attend. One would speculate that attendance would be greater today than in 1963-1964 or 1967-1968, judging by the Gallup attendance trend data, because of increased numbers of black identifiers and, especially, because of the relevancy of the black church as a center of the black community in a postassimilationist period.

The Gallup Organization has occasionally used the survey question: "At the present time do you think religion as a whole is increasing its influence on American Life or losing its influence?" The meaning of this question in the minds of respondents has been questioned. "When black Americans answer this question are they thinking of their own lives and actions, or are they reacting to the apparent influence of professed religion on the actions of whites? Further, are they viewing religion as the churches, specifically, or more broadly as moral values? Whatever its true meaning, the question does not appear to measure amount of influence. *Instead, it may measure perception of change in the religious situation.*"[17] While two-thirds of the black Protestants and slightly less than two-thirds of the white Protestants compared to one-half of the white Catholics felt in March 1967 that religion was losing its influence, by April 1968 the proportion of black Protestants believing it was losing its influence barely declined to slightly less than two-thirds, compared with an increase to three-fourths for white Protestants and to two-thirds for white Catholics. In other words, whites had an increasingly pessimistic view of religion in America (which was probably linked with their decreasing attendance), while the outlook of blacks did not change or even improved very slightly during this short period. In sum, the strength of the black church had improved by the late 1960s, while the strength of white Protestantism and Catholicism had declined in terms of attendance and there was an increased feeling that religion was losing its influence on American life.

### Implications

Black religion is multifaceted, and it cannot be said that black religiosity in general dampens militancy. Orthodoxy, as a churchlike measure for Bowling Green, Kentucky, black residents, is positively rather than inversely related to militancy.[18]

It would appear that black religion and protest are inextricably linked. Drawing heavily from black literary works, Carleton L. Lee develops this thesis, concluding that the link between black religion and protest suggests the black community "for a long time to come, will continue its protest against racial segregation and discrimination as 'devoutly' as the Roman Catholic attends Mass, or as faithfully as the Moslem turns to Mecca to pray.[19]

The close tie between black religion and protest is most evident from a careful reading of Mays and Nicholson's Negro Church. The casual observer of the black church, blinded by a stereotype of black religiosity as generally emotional and otherworldly, expects black sermons to be otherworldly and yet moralistic, aimed at securing heavenly rewards for the followers who firmly hold to simplistic beliefs and who attempt to follow moralistic ethics. Yet Mays and Nicholson startle the reader when they report the results of an analysis of 100 sermons by pastors of churches included in their study. For instance, they write that 54 of the 100 sermons "were highly other-worldly, or at least ended with a distinctly other-world emphasis" and they give as an example the following (here excerpted): "We see the three crosses. The first is of the dying thief. He represents rebellion and stubbornness. . . . This first cross represents those scoffers who are always running down the church. It represents the Negro who will run down his own race, just in order to be able to be noticed by some of the opposite race."[20] The sermon ends, not on the otherworldly note we have been led to expect but with an implication for temporal affairs: "The three crosses are before you today. Are you willing to suffer for Jesus? Do you love him enough to stand by him when the world is against him? Are you repenting of your sins today? Oh, friends, *take the cross of stubbornness out of your life.*"[21] Mays and Nicholson comment, "The other-worldly sermons also reflect the experience of the race. . . . In slightly more than 65 per cent of the this-worldly, and in many of the other-worldly sermons, one is able to glimpse the present social and economic problems that confront the Negro."[22] They conclude that "the emphasis on the other world among Negroes is becoming less and less pronounced."[23]

There is considerable affinity, then, between a religious form which is presumably sectarian and the overcoming of the problems of this world as they are encountered by blacks; perhaps this indicates that this form of religiosity is not as sectarian as supposed. As Yinger writes: "An otherworldly sect may plant seeds of hope which, when the situation changes somewhat, blossom quite rapidly. It is particularly important that the doctrine of a minority sect not be read only on the literal level. There may be deflected and disguised aggression in an accommodative sect; and a doctrine of aggression may serve to hide a program of accommodation."[24]

One is reminded here of one of Marx's militancy items (stated in negative terms, with an endorsement coded as nonmilitant): "Negroes should spend more time praying and less time demonstrating." Yet Marx notes that one clergyman added "Praying is demonstrating."[25] One wonders if Marx fully got the point, or if he misinterpreted the "holy war" as nonmilitant. Brink and Harris may see the situation more clearly:

But from the standpoint of the present revolution, the Negro's religious bent is far less important than the *intensity* of his devotion to Christian ideals. Long dependent on the word of God because he had nothing else, the Negro is today utterly convinced that his cause is just because it is just before God, and that he must ultimately win because that is God's word and will. In a literal sense, his revolution is thus a holy war.

Throughout all of the survey, the Negroes bore testimony to this. Whether the question asked them concerned demonstrations or the outcome of the revolution, many Negroes fell back on their religious faith in answering. "God will find a way for whoever is right," said a 40-year-old domestic in Dallas, Texas. The very strength of the Negro's religion caused a housewife in Atlanta, Georgia, to prophesy, "The Negroes trust and believe in Jesus more than white people do, therefore we will win."[26]

Black religion serves in part as a channel through which feelings about society can be voiced and protest expressed in a routinized way. In his paradigm of the processes of assimilation, Gordon has identified "civic assimilation" as the ultimate form of assimilation and defines this form as the "absence of value and power conflict." In his assessment of black assimilation into American society he partly negates the unidimensionality of the assimilative processes by crediting blacks as being assimilated in the civic sense (but not in terms of most of the other processes.)[27] Using Gordon's framework in his analysis of blacks, Pinkney corrects this attribution of civic assimilation into the white value system by noting that there is an increasing conflict occurring between blacks and whites, for example, over the distribution of power. Yet, on the whole, Pinkney comes to the conclusion that "at the present time there are few areas of value or power conflict between black and white Americans."[28] Assimilationist-oriented researchers have tended to view black religion as otherworldly and as retarding assimilation. Recognition by these scholars of the strong protest motif within black religion would have directed them to question the degree to which black and white Americans share the same goals and values. Our point is simply that protest-oriented black religion calls into question the predominant American value system that has worked to the advantage of whites for so long. Of course the strength of this motif has varied over time.

As assimilation was felt to be taking place, the black church waned; but with growing racial conflict over basic values, the black church has begun to wax once more, since one function of the black church has ever been to call into question the goals of white America.[29] Mays has written that one function of the black church (and the Christian church generally) is "to point out the social implications of the religion of Jesus. . . . It is not enough for the church to give lip service to the doctrine of the Fatherhood of God and the brotherhood of men [but] it must seek progressively to implement the doctrine at the risk of peril into every phase of human endeavor."[30]

# APPENDIXES

# A:

## Bowling Green Sample

In this appendix the sampling technique for securing interviews with black residents of Bowling Green, Kentucky, will be briefly described. The population sampled was defined as all black adults (18 years and older) who were permanent residents of Bowling Green as of October 1, 1970. "Permanent resident" was defined as an individual who indicated that he regarded only Bowling Green as his place of residence; this excluded most students attending Western Kentucky University.

An intense effort was made to compile a population listing including all black households in Bowling Green. Since most black families live within the Bowling Green Model Cities target area, an initial list of all households in that area was compiled from the 1969 *Bowling Green City Directory*.[1] Since the city directory was somewhat incomplete, additional households were added to the list from specific counts of housing units not listed in the directory. Approximately 40 percent of the Model Cities target area is black. In addition to the Model Cities target area, there are two additional, rather small, enclaves of blacks outside the area. The housing in these areas was added to the list of housing units.

Because sampling of housing units in the areas specified drew whites, as well as blacks, four independent, systematic random samples of 321 respondents (320 for the fourth wave) were drawn from the Model Cities area, resulting in a total N of 1,323. An additional 40 respondents were drawn for black areas outside the Model Cities area. Prior to the sampling, estimates for percent black were made; and the sample was drawn to yield about 400 black households. Of the total number, 228 were individuals who fell outside the population definition and 418 were black households. A technique for randomly drawing a member of each household was used to randomize selection of individual respondents.[2] This technique depends on the full enumeration of adult household members by the initial person contacted and on full cooperation of the interviewer in making repeated callbacks to secure the interview from the selected respondent.

Black interviewers were used to interview black respondents. The race of each prospective respondent was first identified. An in-depth callback procedure was used which meant that callbacks were continued until every prospective respondent was contacted. For the black sample, no prospective respondent was missed. Of the 418 individuals there were 12 outright refusals and 1 incomplete interview schedule, resulting in 405 completed interviews, with a resulting 96.9 percent completion rate.

Interviewing was begun in the middle of October, 1970. Approximately one-half of the black sample had been interviewed by mid-December, 1970, and about two-thirds had been interviewed by the end of February, 1971. The callback process continued until all prospective sample members had been reached, a procedure which was completed at the end of May, 1971. Although the interviewing was continued for several months, there is no reason for assuming that any important variables would evidence short-run changes. Interviewing was called off in the Christmas and Easter periods in order to diminish the problems associated with higher rates of church attendance during the religious holiday seasons.

Interviewers were fully trained in the use of the schedule. Following the pretest of the schedule in a neighboring community, in which students were used as interviewers, it was decided not to use students for survey interviewing. Instead, interviewers came from several referral sources, including the local Economic Security Office and through advertisements in the local newspaper. Most interviewers resided in the Model Cities target area and had a good working knowledge of the area. During the process of interviewing, schedules were checked as they came in; and additional interviewer training occurred when a check of the completed interviews indicated that this was necessary. Spot checking by telephone was done on every interviewer in order to weed out interviews and inter-

Table 45

Percentage Distribution of Age of Head of Household,
Bowling Green Blacks, Sample and Census Data

| Population | N | 24 and under | 25-34 | 35-44 | 45-64 | 65 and over |
|-----------|-----|------|------|------|------|------|
| 1970 Census | 1,048 | 7.9 | 15.7 | 17.3 | 37.5 | 21.6 |
| Survey | 245 | 10.2 | 17.1 | 15.9 | 35.1 | 21.6 |

NOTE: Chi-square=2.01 d.f.=4 P>.05. Due to rounding the total percentage does not always equal 100.0.

viewers who were "curbstoning," or filling out interview schedules without really interviewing (this occurred in only two instances). The time per schedule averaged one hour and three-quarters.

With the completion, including coding, of the white interview schedules, a full comparison of survey and general population characteristics using 1970 census data will be made. Of the 405 respondents, 64.4 percent were female, while a preliminary check indicates that about 55 percent should be female. This bias, due in part to interviewers not calling back as often as they should have and, instead, interviewing an adult female, would not introduce significant bias into the sample, especially since sex of the respondent is always controlled in the analysis of the data.

Table 45 reports the percentage distribuiton of the age of head of household for the survey data and for the 1970 census data.[3] The percentages are strikingly similar, lending confidence to the representativeness of the sample.

Finally a brief comment should be made about the city of Bowling Green. As reported in the 1970 Census, Bowling Green has a population of 36,253 of which 3,697, or 10.2 percent, are black. Bowling Green, the county seat of Warren County, is located in the south central part of Kentucky and is 114 miles south of Louisville and 61 miles north of Nashville. Warren County, with a population of 57,432 in 1970, of which 8.6 percent are nonwhite, is the leading county of Kentucky in milk production. Bowling Green, a tobacco-growing marketing center, is diversified in terms of light industries, including garment and automobile parts manufacturing plants.[4]

# B:

## Data Sets Used in This Study

The following Gallup data sets were employed in this study. Also given is the size of sample and the variable under study.

AIPO 539, November 1954, N=1,459 (129 nonwhite, 1,276 white, 54 no response). This data set was employed for racial differences on the intellectual dimension of religiosity.

AIPO 580, March 1957, N=1,629 (172 nonwhite, 1,457 white). Ideological dimension, involuntary characteristic, church addressing social and political questions.

AIPO 625, February 1960, N=2,998 (372 black, 2,603 white, 7 other nonwhite). Attendance trends.

AIPO 642, March 1961, N=3,510 (375 black, 3,135 white). Attendance trends.

AIPO 655, February 1962, N=2,993 (312 black, 2,658 white, 23 other nonwhite). Experiential dimension.

AIPO 658, May 1962, N=3,659 (399 black, 3,253 white, 7 other nonwhite). Attendance trends.

AIPO 660, June 1962, N=3,275 (283 black, 2,989 white, 2 other nonwhite). Attendance trends.

AIPO 673, May 1963, N=4,133 (485 black, 3,636 white, 12 other nonwhite). Attitude toward King, attendance trends.

AIPO 676, August 1963, N=3,555 (449 black, 3,092 white, 14 other nonwhite). March on Washington, attendance trends.

AIPO 681, December 1963, N=4429 (629 black, 3,788 white, 12 other nonwhite). Ritualistic dimension: prayer; ritualistic dimension: attendance; involuntary characteristic; attendance trends.

AIPO 695, July 1964, N=3,513 (397 black, 3,066 white, 50 other nonwhite). Attendance trends.

AIPO 706, February 1965, N=1,571 (141 black, 1,412 white, 17 other nonwhite). Attendance trends.

AIPO 708, March 1965, N=3,500 (403 black, 3,066 white, 31 other nonwhite). Attitude toward clergy protesting.

AIPO 710, April 1965, N=3,499 (374 black, 3,111 white, 14 other nonwhite). Attendance trends.

AIPO 711, May 1965, N=3,509 (455 black, 3,034 white, 20 other nonwhite). Attitude toward King.

AIPO 734, September 1966, N=1,554 (125 black, 1,409 white, 20 other nonwhite). Attendance trends.

AIPO 738, December 1966, N=1,467 (141 black, 1,310 white, 16 other nonwhite). Attendance trends.

AIPO 742, March 1967, N=3,521 (279 black, 3,212 white, 30 other nonwhite). Religion's influence.

AIPO 749, August 1967, N=3,552 (294 black, 3,234 white, 23 other nonwhite). Attendance trends.

AIPO 757, January 1968, N=1,500 (92 black, 1,394 white, 14 other nonwhite). Attendance trends.

AIPO 758, February 1968, N=1,501 (111 black, 1,378 white, 12 other nonwhite). Church addressing social and political questions.

AIPO 760, April 1968, N=1,504 (86 black, 1,407 white, 11 other nonwhite). Attendance trends; religion's influence.

AIPO 764, June 1968, N=1,537 (123 black, 1,407 white, 7 other nonwhite). Ideological dimension; ritualistic dimension: attendance; attendance trends.

AIPO 766, August 1968, N=1,526 (123 black, 1,399 white, 4 other nonwhite). Attendance trends.

AIPO 780, May 1969, N=1,523 (120 black, 1,393 white, 10 other nonwhite). Ritualistic dimension: attendance; attendance trends.

AIPO 781, May 1969, N=1,538 (110 black, 1,412 white, 16 other nonwhite). Ritualistic dimension: attendance; attendance trends.

The other data sets employed in this study were:

Detroit Area Study 849, Gerhard Lenski, Director, 1958 Survey. Attendance and devotionalism.

New York City, Public Images of Mental Health Services Study,

1963-1964. Minority group self-identification and attendance.
Negro Political Attitudes, Gary T. Marx, 1964, N=1,119 (black). Religiosity and militancy.
Bowling Green, Kentucky, Black Church As a Politicizing Agency, 1970-1971, N=405 (black). Religiosity and militancy.

# NOTES

## Chapter 1

1. Donald Young, *American Minority Peoples* (New York: Harper and Brothers, 1932), p. 526.

2. Peter H. Rossi, "New Directions for Race Relations Research in the Sixties," *Review of Religious Research* 5 (Spring 1964):129-31.

3. L. Paul Metzger, "American Sociology and Black Assimilation: Conflicting Perspectives," *American Journal of Sociology* 76(January 1971):629, 639.

4. Michael Argyle, "Religious Observance," *International Encyclopedia of the Social Sciences*, ed. David L. Sills (New York: Macmillan, 1968), 13:425.

5. Charles F. Marden and Gladys Meyer, *Minorities in American Society* 2d ed. (New York: American Book Company, 1962), p. 244.

6. On black membership see Harry V. Richardson, "The Negro in American Religious Life," *The American Negro Reference Book*, ed. John P. Davis (Englewood Cliffs, N.J.:Prentice-Hall, 1966), p. 402.

7. Samuel S. Hill, *Southern Churches in Crisis* (New York: Holt, Rinehart, and Winston, 1967), p. 25.

8. Hart M. Nelsen and Raytha L. Yokley, "Presbyterians, Civil Rights and Church Pronouncements," *Review of Religious Research* 12 (Fall 1970):43.

9. Phillip E. Hammond and Robert E. Mitchell, "Segmentation of Radicalism—the Case of the Protestant Campus Minister," *American Journal of Sociology* 71 (September 1965):135.

10. Arthur Fauset, *Black Gods of the Metropolis* (Philadelphia: University of Pennsylvania Press, 1944), p. 109; also in Hart M. Nelsen, Raytha L. Yokley, and Anne K. Nelsen, eds., *The Black Church in America* (New York: Basic Books, 1971), p. 172.

11. For contradictory evidence on the part of black clergy, see Hart M. Nelsen, Raytha L. Yokley, and Thomas W. Madron, "Ministerial Roles and Social Actionist Stance: Protestant Clergy and Protest in the Sixties," *American Sociological Review* 38 (June 1973):384.

12. John B. Holt, "Holiness Religion: Cultural Shock and Social Reorganization," *American Sociological Review* 5 (October 1940):740-47.

13. Hart M. Nelsen, Raytha L. Yokley, and Thomas W. Madron, "Rural-Urban Differences in Religiosity," *Rural Sociology* 36 (September 1971):392.

14. Holt, "Holiness Religion," p. 741.

147

15. Russell R. Dynes, "Rurality, Migration, and Sectarianism," *Rural Sociology* 21 (March 1956):28.

16. Hart M. Nelsen and Hugh P. Whitt, "Religion and the Migrant in the City: A Test of Holt's Cultural Shock Thesis," *Social Forces* 50 (March 1972):379-84; see also Hart M. Nelsen, "Sectarianism, World View, and Anomie," *Social Forces* 51 (December 1972): 226-33.

17. Alphonso Pinkney, *Black Americans* (Englewood Cliffs, N.J.: Prentice-Hall, 1969), p. 110.

18. Young, *American Minority Peoples*, pp. 534-35.

19. E. Franklin Frazier, *The Negro Church in America* (New York: Schocken Books, 1964), p. 71; also in H. Nelsen, Yokley, and A. Nelsen, *Black Church in America*, p. 134.

20. Young, *American Minority Peoples*, pp. 534-35.

21. For the dual role of religion as opiate or inspiration of militancy, see: Vincent Harding, "Religion and Resistance among Antebellum Negroes, 1800-1860," in *The Making of Black America*, ed. August Meier and Elliott Rudwick, 2 vols. (New York: Atheneum, 1969), 1:179-97; Gary T. Marx, "Religion: Opiate or Inspiration of Civil Rights Militancy among Negroes?" *American Sociological Review* 32 (February 1967):64-72; Clifton F. Brown, "Black Religion—1968," in *In Black America, 1968: The Year of Awakening*, ed. Patricia W. Romero (Washington, D. C.: United Publishing Corporation for the Association for the Study of Negro Life and History, Pioneer Paperbook, 1969), pp. 345-53, and also in H. Nelsen, Yokley, and A. Nelsen, *Black Church in America*, pp. 17-28; LeRoy Moore, Jr., "The Spiritual: Soul of Black Religion," *American Quarterly* 23 (December 1971):658-76.

22. Robert E. Lane, *Political Life: Why People Get Involved in Politics*, (New York: Free Press of Glencoe, 1959), pp. 245, 251.

23. Ibid., p. 255.

24. Raymond Breton, "Institutional Completeness of Ethnic Communities and the Personal Relations of Immigrants," *American Journal of Sociology* 70 (September 1964):197.

25. Ibid., p. 199.

26. Ibid., pp. 200-201.

27. Ibid., p. 204.

28. Ibid., p. 205.

29. James S. Coleman, *Resources for Social Change* (New York: John Wiley & Sons, 1971), p. 18.

30. Ibid., p. 22.

31. For a selection of his sermons, see Albert B. Cleage, Jr., *The Black Messiah* (New York: Sheed and Ward, 1968).

32. Frazier, *The Negro Church in America*, pp. 78-81, 85-86.

33. Anthony M. Orum, "A Reappraisal of the Social and Political Participation of Negroes," *American Journal of Sociology* 72 (July 1966):33.

34. Charles E. Silberman, *Crisis in Black and White* (New York: Random House, 1964), p. 144. It might be noted that the inverse relationship between class and organizational membership was reported by Wright and Hyman. See: Charles R. Wright and Herbert H. Hyman, "Voluntary Association Memberships of American Adults: Evidence from National Sample Surveys." *American Sociological Review* 23 (June 1958):284-94; Herbert H. Hyman and Charles R. Wright, "Trends in Voluntary Association Memberships of American Adults: Replication Based on Secondary Analysis of National

Sample Surveys," *American Sociological Review* 36 (April 1971):191-206.

35. St. Clair Drake and Horace Cayton, *Black Metropolis*, 2 vols. (New York: Harper & Row, 1945), 2:424.

36. Gunnar Myrdal, *An American Dilemma* (New York: Harper & Row, 1944), p. 928. Italics are Myrdal's.

37. Ibid., pp. 952-53.

38. See, for example, Orum, "A Reappraisal of the Social and Political Participation of Negroes," pp. 32-46; Marvin E. Olsen, "Social and Political Participation of Blacks," *American Sociological Review* 35 (August 1970):682-97. We have elaborated our own position on the church as a voluntary association elsewhere; see H. Nelsen, Yokley, and A. Nelsen, *Black Church in America*, pp. 10, 12.

39. Nicholas Babchuk and Ralph Thompson, "The Voluntary Associations of Negroes," *American Sociologicl Review* 27 (October 1962):648, 654-55. Babchuk reported that 87.5 percent of their sample of Lincoln, Nebraska, blacks had religious affiliations. They lacked data on whites residing in the same locale and so their comparisons were to data from national surveys, especially a study by Wright and Hyman which was reported in 1958. These researchers found membership in voluntary associations (with churches excluded) was more characteristic of whites than of blacks, with 46 percent of the former and 60 percent of the latter of a 1953 national survey belonging to no organization (see Wright and Hyman, "Voluntary Association Memberships," pp. 287, 294). In a later analysis, published in 1971, Wright and Hyman reported a "sharp increase" in black membership. Among their conclusions: the majority of Americans still do not belong to voluntary associations; increases in membership have taken place at all class levels; and increased membership was more characteristic of blacks than whites, thus reducing the gap noted in their 1958 publication (see "Trends," pp. 203, 205).

Orum noted that Wright and Hyman did not control for social class, thus "obscuring membership rates of whites and Negroes at comparable socioeconomic levels." From analyses of several sets of data, Orum had concluded that "among Negroes and whites at the lower-class level, the Negroes were more likely to be affiliated with organizations." Blacks were more likely to belong to political and church groups than whites (with socioeconomic status held constant), and were as likely to belong to civic groups. As a consequence of this finding, Orum rejected the isolationist view and affirmed Myrdal's interpretation (see Orum, "A Reappraisal," pp. 35, 45).

Finally, it should be noted that Hyman and Wright ("Trends," pp. 202-3) reported why they did not control on socioeconomic status: "A configuration of handicaps is part of the distinctive social plight of American Negroes. To compare them with that unusual group of whites who are characterized by the same handicaps or disadvantages would hardly present a faithful description of social reality."

40. Myrdal, *An American Dilemma*, pp. 873, 757.

41. Ibid., p. 877.

42. An extended discussion of the Mays and Nicholson study and its implications for the rural and urban incarnations of the church appears in chapter 3.

43. Benjamin E. Mays and Joseph W. Nicholson, *The Negro's Church* (New York: Institute of Social and Religious Research, 1933), p. 278; also in H. Nelsen, Yokley, and A. Nelsen, *Black Church in America*, pp. 287-88.

44. Olsen, "Social and Political Participation of Blacks," p. 696. It can be noted that Hyman and Wright ("Trends," p. 202) commented on the decreasing white-black gap in membership rates by referring to the blacks' lessening fear of reprisals from whites against their organization efforts. Such fears were reduced by the ideological currents of the past decade, according to the authors.

45. Mays and Nicholson, *Negro's Church*, pp. 279-84, 291-92.

46. Joseph R. Washington, Jr., *The Politics of God* (Boston: Beacon Press, 1967), pp. 226-27.

47. Joseph R. Washington, Jr., *Black Religion* (Boston: Beacon Press, 1964), p. 289.

48. Gayraud S. Wilmore, Jr., "The Case for a New Black Church Style," *Church in Metropolis* 18 (Fall 1968):18; also in H. Nelsen, Yokley, and A. Nelsen, *Black Church in America*, p. 325.

49. Wilmore, "Case," p. 20; also in H. Nelsen, Yokley, and A. Nelsen, *Black Church in America*, p. 328.

50. George Eaton Simpson, "Assimilation," *International Encyclopedia of the Social Sciences*, 1:438.

51. Ibid.

52. Milton M. Gordon, *Assimilation in American Life* (New York: Oxford University Press, 1964), pp. 67, 71.

53. Ibid., p. 79.

54. On migration and increasing education levels, see: St. Clair Drake, "The Social and Economic Status of the Negro in the United States," in *The Negro American*, ed. Talcott Parsons and Kenneth B. Clark (Boston: Beacon Press, 1967). pp. 3-46; Philip M. Hauser, "Demographic Factors in the Integration of the Negro," in *The Negro American*, pp. 71-101; Norval D. Glenn, "Changes in the Social and Economic Conditions of Black Americans during the 1960's," in *Blacks in the United States*, ed. Norval D. Glenn and Charles M. Bonjean (San Francisco: Chandler Publishing Company, 1969), pp. 43-54; Leonard Broom and Norval Glenn, *Transformation of the Negro American* (New York: Harper and Row, 1965), pp. 81-104; and Reynolds Farley, "The Urbanization of Negroes in the United States," *Journal of Social History* 1 (Spring 1968):241-58.

55. Gary T. Marx, *Protest and Prejudice*, rev. ed. (New York: Harper & Row, 1969), p. 105; also in H. Nelsen, Yokley, and A. Nelsen, *Black Church in America*, p. 158.

56. Gordon notes that structural assimilation did not occur to any great degree. "To understand, then, that acculturation without massive structural intermingling at primary group levels has been the dominant motif in the American experience of creating and developing a nation out of diverse peoples is to comprehend the most essential sociological fact of that experience." *Assimilation in American Life*, p. 114.

### Chapter 2

1. Kenneth M. Stampp, *The Peculiar Institution: Slavery in the Ante-Bellum South* (New York: Alfred A. Knopf, 1956), p. 161; also in Hart M. Nelsen, Raytha L. Yokley, and Anne K. Nelsen, eds., *The Black Church in America* (New York: Basic Books, 1971), p. 57.

2. For a description of a white-conducted slave service, see Clifton H.

Johnson, ed., *God Struck Me Dead* (Philadelphia: United Church Press, 1969), pp. 134-35.

3. E. Franklin Frazier, *The Negro Church in America* (New York: Schocken Books, 1964), p. 19.

4. Richard C. Wade, *Slavery in the Cities: The South 1820-1860* (New York: Oxford University Press, 1964), p. 162; also in H. Nelsen, Yokley, and A. Nelsen, *Black Church in America*, p. 65.

5. Wade, *Slavery in the Cities*, p. 166; also in H. Nelsen, Yokley, and A. Nelsen, *Black Church in America*, p. 67.

6. Wade, *Slavery in the Cities*, p. 168; also in H. Nelsen, Yokley, and A. Nelsen, *Black Church in America*, p. 69; see also Vincent Harding, "Religion and Resistance among Antebellum Negroes, 1800-1860," in *The Orgins of Black America*, vol. 1, in *The Making of Black America*, ed. August Meier and Elliott Rudwick (New York: Atheneum, 1969), pp. 184-85; Gayraud S. Wilmore, *Black Religion and Black Radicalism* (Garden City, N. Y.: Doubleday & Co., 1972), pp. 79-84.

7. Wade, *Slavery in the Cities*, p. 171; also in H. Nelsen, Yokley, and A. Nelsen, *Black Church in America*, p. 70.

8. John Hope Franklin, *From Slavery to Freedom: a History of Negro Americans*, 3d ed. (New York: Alfred A. Knopf, 1967), pp. 108-9.

9. Lorenzo Johnston Greene, *The Negro in Colonial New England* (New York: Columbia University Press, 1942), p. 285.

10. Winthrop D. Jordan, *White over Black: American Attitudes toward the Negro, 1550-1812* (Chapel Hill: University of North Carolina Press for the Institute of Early American History and Culture, 1968), pp. 422-26; also in H. Nelsen, Yokley, and A. Nelsen, *Black Church in America*, pp. 49-52.

11. Leon F. Litwack, *North of Slavery: The Negro in the Free States 1790-1860* (Chicago and London: University of Chicago Press, 1961), p. 195.

12. Franklin, *From Slavery to Freedom*, p. 227.

13. W. E. Burghardt Du Bois, *The Souls of Black Folk: Essays and Sketches* (Chicago: A. C. McClurg & Company, 1903), p. 144; also in H. Nelsen, Yokley, and A. Nelsen, *Black Church in America*, p. 33.

14. Du Bois, *Souls of Black Folk*, pp. 144-47; also in H. Nelsen, Yokley, and A. Nelsen, *Black Church in America*, pp. 33-35.

15. Du Bois, *Souls of Black Folk*, p. 148; also in H. Nelsen, Yokley, and A. Nelsen, *Black Church in America*, p. 36.

16. Melville J. Herskovits, *The Myth of the Negro Past* (New York: Harper & Row, 1941), pp. 208, 232-33; also in H. Nelsen, Yokley, and A. Nelsen, *Black Church in America*, pp. 46-47.

17. Frazier, *Negro Church*, p. 6.

18. Ibid., pp. 8-9.

19. Ibid., pp. 12, 16, 19.

20. Harding, "Religion and Resistance," pp. 184-85.

21. Ibid., pp. 190-95, 197. For an extended discussion of slave religion and spirituals in terms of the functions of release from despair and the expression of the desire for freedom, see John W. Blassingame, *The Slave Community* (New York: Oxford University Press, 1972), pp. 64-76.

22. Jon Butler, "Communities and Congregations: The Black Church in St. Paul, 1860-1900," *Journal of Negro History* 56 (April 1971): 118-34.

23. S. P. Fullinwider, *The Mind and Mood of Black America* (Homewood, Ill.: Dorsey Press, 1969).

24. Carter G. Woodson, *The History of the Negro Church*, 2d ed. (Washington, D. C.: Associated Publishers, 1921).

25. Frazier, *Negro Church*, p. 29.

26. Woodson, *History*, pp. 188-92.

27. Ibid., pp. 196-98.

28. Ibid., p. 199.

29. Ibid., pp. 200-201.

30. The following discussion is based on Woodson, *History*, chap.12.

31. Ibid., p. 250.

32. Ibid., p. 291.

33. Frazier, *Negro Church*, p. 5.

34. Ibid., p. 30.

35. W. E. Burghardt Du Bois, *The Philadelphia Negro: A Social Study* (Philadelphia: Published for the University of Pennsylvania, 1899), pp. 203-4; also in H. Nelsen, Yokley, and A. Nelsen, *Black Church in America*, pp. 78-79.

36. Butler, "Communities and Congregations," p. 125.

37. Frazier, *Negro Church*, pp. 32-33.

38. Du Bois, *Philadelphia Negro*, pp. 206-7.

39. Booker T. Washington, "The Religious Life of the Negro," *North American Review* 159 (July 1905): 22; also in H. Nelsen, Yokley, and A. Nelsen, *Black Church in America*, p. 42.

40. Woodson, *History*, p. 203.

41. Ibid., p. 205.

42. Ibid., pp. 216-17.

43. August Meier, *Negro Thought in America, 1880-1915: Racial Ideologies in the Age of Booker T. Washington* (Ann Arbor: University of Michigan Press, 1963), pp. 245-46.

44. Frazier, *Negro Church*, pp. 42, 40. Julius Rosenwald (1862-1932), an American merchant and philanthropist, made major contributions for the improvement of southern black educational facilities. See Franklin, *From Slavery to Freedom*, pp. 385, 547-48.

45. Ibid., p. 35.

46. Ibid., p. 36.

47. Ibid., pp. 37-38.

48. Du Bois, *Philadelphia Negro*, pp. 207-21.

49. Gilbert Osofsky, *Harlem: The Making of a Ghetto: Negro New York, 1890-1930*, 2d ed. (New York: Harper & Row, Torchbook, 1971), p. 115.

50. Ibid., pp. 115-17.

51. Woodson, *History*, pp. 220-22.

52. Ibid., pp. 223-46.

53. Butler, "Communities and Congregations," p. 132.

54. Meier, *Negro Thought*, pp. 218-19.

55. Ibid., pp. 220-22.

56. Ibid., pp. 223-24.

57. Fullinwinder, *Mind and Mood*, pp. 29-30.

58. Actually a loss of confidence in white America and a new militant black nationalism were highly visible in the person of Henry McNeal Turner, who became a bishop in the A. M. E. church in 1880 with the support of other dissident black Methodists of the South. Turner's separatism and early demands for reparations for the enslavement of blacks set him apart from most other activists of his time, though not from Marcus Garvey and the black

nationalists of the twentieth century. See Wilmore, *Black Religion*, pp. 168-76.

59. Fullinwider, *Mind and Mood*, pp. 33-36, 41.

60. Ibid., p. 46; also note Woodson, *History*, pp. 305-7.

## Chapter 3

1. John Hope Franklin, *From Slavery to Freedom: A History of Negro Americans*, 3d ed. (New York: Alfred A. Knopf, 1967), pp. 471-83.

2. Benjamin E. Mays and Joseph W. Nicholson, *The Negro's Church* (New York: Institute of Social and Religious Research, 1933), pp. 96, 231, 259, 261, 274.

3. Ibid., p. 277.

4. Ibid., pp. 254-57.

5. Charles S. Johnson, *Growing Up in the Black Belt* (Washington, D. C.: American Council on Education, 1941), p. 169; also in Hart M. Nelsen, Raytha L. Yokley, and Anne K. Nelsen, eds., *The Black Church in America* (New York: Basic Books, 1971), p. 99.

6. Johnson, *Growing Up in the Black Belt*, pp. 158, 146-54; also in H. Nelsen, Yokley, and A. Nelsen, *Black Church in America*, pp. 98, 96-97.

7. Johnson, *Growing Up in the Black Belt*, pp. 145-46, 169; also in H. Nelsen, Yokley, and A. Nelsen, *Black Church in America*, pp. 96, 99.

8. Ibid.

9. Harry V. Richardson, *Dark Glory: A Picture of the Church among Negroes in the Rural South* (New York: Published for Home Missions Council of North America and Phelps-Stokes Fund by Friendship Press, 1947), p. 93.

10. Ibid., pp. 34-49.

11. Ibid., p. 139. In 1949 an additional survey of the rural church was undertaken on a much larger scale than ever before by Ralph A. Felton of the Rural Church Department of Drew Theological Seminary, Madison, New Jersey, under the sponsorship of the Home Missions Council of North America and the Phelps-Stokes Fund. Harry V. Richardson, president of Gammon Theological Seminary, Atlanta, Georgia, served as consultant to the project. The study involved a survey of 1,542 black homes in 12 counties and of 570 black churches in 17 counties of the South. The Felton study contains valuable statistics on everything from membership percentages among black owners and tenants to community organizations to which the pastor belongs, to distances from the black home to such community services as the church, high school, and hospital. Much as his predecessors had, however, Felton found a church which was declining and gravely in need of a new type of pastor to provide community leadership. Felton thus offers little that is new in theory or interpretation of the rural black church, but supplies a breadth and quanity of very useful supporting data to the findings made earlier on a more limited scale by Mays and Nicholson, and, especially, Harry Richardson. The Felton study is entitled *These My Brethren: A Study of 570 Negro Churches and 1542 Negro Homes in the Rural South*.

12. Hylan Lewis, *Blackways of Kent* (Chapel Hill: University of North Carolina Press, 1955). p. 130 (pagination from 1964 paperback edition published by the College and University Press, New Haven); also in H. Nelsen, Yokley, and A. Nelsen, *Black Church in America*, pp. 106-7.

13. H. Nelsen, Yokley, and A. Nelsen, *Black Church in America*, p. 10.

14. Lewis, *Blackways of Kent*, p. 27.
15. Ibid., pp. 137-39; also in H. Nelsen, Yokley, and A. Nelsen, *Black Church in America*, pp. 106-7.
16. Richard C. Wade, *Slavery in the Cities: The South 1820-1860* (New York: Oxford University Press, 1964), pp. 169-71; also in H. Nelsen, Yokley, and A. Nelsen, *Black Church in America*, pp. 69-71.
17. Lewis, *Blackways of Kent*, p. 148; also in H. Nelsen, Yokley, and A. Nelsen, *Black Church in America*, p. 108.
18. Lewis, *Blackways of Kent*, p. 148; also in H. Nelsen, Yokley, and A. Nelsen, *Black Church in America*, p. 113.
19. Lewis, *Blackways of Kent*, pp. 276-77.
20. Ibid., pp. 241-42.
21. Mays and Nicholson, *Negro's Church*, pp. 96-97.
22. Ibid., p. 113.
23. Ibid., pp. 122-23.
24. Ibid., p. 17.
25. Ibid., p. 100.
26. Ibid., pp. 173, 171.
27. Ibid., pp. 180-81.
28. Ibid., table XVI, p. 218.
29. Ibid., pp. 216, 227-28.
30. Allan H. Spear, *Black Chicago: The Making of a Negro Ghetto 1890-1920* (Chicago and London: University of Chicago Press, 1967), pp. 53, 91.
31. Ibid., pp. 91-93, 95-97.
32. Ibid., p. 179.
33. Vattel Elbert Daniel, "Ritual and Stratification in Chicago Negro Churches," *American Sociological Review* 7 (June 1942): 354; also in H. Nelsen, Yokley, and A. Nelsen, *Black Church in America*, p. 121.
34. Daniel, "Ritual and Stratification," pp. 358-59; also in H. Nelsen, Yokley, and A. Nelsen, *Black Church in America*, p. 126.
35. Daniel, "Ritual and Stratification," p. 361; also in H. Nelsen, Yokley, and A. Nelsen, *Black Church in America*, pp. 128-29.
36. St. Clair Drake and Horace R. Cayton, *Black Metropolis: A Study of Negro Life in a Northern City*, rev. ed., 2 vols. (New York: Harcourt, Brace & World, 1970), 2:540.
37. Ibid., pp. 684-87, 679-82, 673-79.
38. Ibid., p. 412. Even Mays and Nicholson (*Negro's Church*, p. 59) noted that though the urban ministers tended to be less otherworldly than their rural counterparts, fully 54 of 100 sample urban sermons were otherworldly (but see our comment on this point in chapter 7).
39. Drake and Cayton, *Black Metropolis*, 2:413.
40. Ibid., p. 418.
41. Ibid., pp. 418-19.
42. Ibid., pp. 422-28.
43. Mays and Nicholson, *Negro's Church*, pp. 97-98.
44. Drake and Cayton, *Black Metropolis*, 2:636. After revisiting Bronzeville in 1961, Drake and Cayton noted that the storefront was encountering increasing difficulties: "Store-front churches flourish, but illiterate and semi-literate individuals who feel that they are 'called to preach' find it increasingly

difficult to rent stores, since run-down business streets are being eliminated by slum clearance, and low-cost housing projects make no such provision for such spiritual entrepreneurs. There has been a substantial increase, however, in the number of conventional churches catering to lower-class religious tastes." Drake and Cayton, *Black Metropolis*, 2:xix, xx.

45. Ira E. Harrison, "The Storefront Church as a Revitalization Movement," *Review of Religious Research* 7 (Spring 1966):161; also in H. Nelsen, Yokley, and A. Nelsen, *Black Church in America*, p. 242.

46. Anthony F. C. Wallace, "Revitalization Movements," *American Anthropologist* 58 (April 1956): 264-81.

47. Harrison, "Storefront Church," p. 162; also in H. Nelsen, Yokley, and A. Nelsen, *Black Church in America*, p. 244.

48. For an analysis of pertinent white data, see Hart M. Nelsen and Hugh P. Whitt, "Religion and the Migrant in the City: A Test of Holt's Cultural Shock Thesis," *Social Forces* 50 (March 1972): 379-84.

49. Arthur Huff Fauset, *Black Gods of the Metropolis: Negro Religious Cults of the Urban North* (Philadelphia: University of Pennsylvania Press, 1944), p. 111; also in H. Nelsen, Yokley, and A. Nelsen, *Black Church in America*, p. 167.

50. Fauset, *Black Gods*, pp. 99-100; also in H. Nelsen, Yokley, and A. Nelsen, *Black Church in America*, pp. 166-67.

51. Hadley Cantril and Muzafer Sherif, "The Kingdom of Father Divine," *Journal of Abnormal and Social Psychology* 33 (1938):164, 151-53; also in H. Nelsen, Yokley, and A. Nelsen, *Black Church in America*, pp. 190, 179-80. Also see the discusssion of Father Divine in Fauset, *Black Gods*, pp. 52-67.

52. Howard M. Brotz, "Negro 'Jews' in the United States," *Phylon* 13 (December 1952):329-30; also in H. Nelsen, Yokley, and A. Nelsen, *Black Church in America*, p. 200.

53. Brotz, "Negro Jews," pp. 335-37; also in H. Nelsen, Yokley, and A. Nelsen, *Black Church in America*, pp. 205, 207. A variant group of black Jews is discussed in Fauset, *Black Gods*, pp. 31-40.

54. C. Eric Lincoln, "The Black Muslims As a Protest Movement," in *Assuring Freedom to the Free*, ed. Arnold Rose (Detroit: Wayne State University Press, 1964), pp. 238-40; also in H. Nelsen, Yokley, and A. Nelsen, *Black Church in America*, pp. 222-23.

55. Lincoln, "Black Muslims," p. 229; also in H. Nelsen, Yokley, and A. Nelsen, *Black Church in America*, p. 216.

56. Mays and Nicholson, *Negro's Church*, p. 278.

57. Ibid., pp. 279-84.

58. Ibid., pp. 291-92.

59. Gunnar Myrdal, *An American Dilemma*, (New York: McGraw-Hill Book Co., 1964), p. 867.

60. Ibid., pp. 873-75.

61. Ibid., pp. 873-77.

62. Frazier, *Negro Church in America*, pp. 51, 55.

63. Ibid., pp. 70-71.

64. Ibid., pp. 52, 79-81, 73.

65. Ibid., pp. 85-86. References to pages 68-81 may also be found in H. Nelsen, Yokley, and A. Nelsen, *Black Church in America*, pp. 131-42.

66. One effect of migration and acculturation was conversion to Cath-

olicism; see Hart M. Nelsen and Lynda Dickson, "Attitudes of Black Catholics and Protestants: Evidence for Religious Identity," *Sociological Analysis* 33 (Fall 1972):154.

## Chapter 4

1. Mutiple Classification Analysis, described in Frank Andrews, James Morgan, and John Sonquist, *Multiple Classification Analysis* (Ann Arbor: University of Michigan, Institute for Social Research, 1967), is an analogue of multiple regression analysis. It permits examining the interrelationships among several predictor variables and a dependent variable, assuming an additive model. Predictors can be at less than ordinal measurement; the dependent variable should be at the interval level of measurement or should be dichotomous. From the output one can see the effects of each predictor on the dependent variable, before and after adjusting for the effects of the other predictors. The chief advantage of MCA is that the effects of several variables can be examined at one time, unlike simpler forms of multivariate analysis which generally involve controlling on only one variable in a given analysis run.

Besides producing the unadjusted means (or proportions if the dependent variable is dichotomous and is coded 0 and 1) by categories of the predictor variables, the MCA program gives deviations from the overall mean by categories of the predictor variables, both before and after adjusting for the effects of the other predictors. Andrews, Morgan, and Sonquist *(Multiple Classification Analysis*, p. 128) recommend that the reader be presented with results not in the form of deviations but in the form of unadjusted and adjusted subgroup averages. (Where more than coefficients are presented in this study, this has been the method of presentation adopted.)

The MCA program computes eta (a zero-order correlation ratio) and beta coefficients (the latter is a partial coefficient explaining variation in the dependent variable after the effects of all other predictors are adjusted). From a visual inspection of the means across categories of a predictor, the sign of the coefficient can be determined. Finally, the program produces a multiple (R) correlation coefficient, as well as sums of squares for computing significance levels.

The reader desiring more information on MCA as well as other applications should see, in addition to the Andrews, Morgan, and Sonquist volume, the following: Peter M. Blau and Otis Dudley Duncan, *The American Occupational Structure* (New York: John Wiley & Sons, 1967), pp. 128-40; Jerald G. Bachman, *Youth in Transition*, vol. 2, *The Impact of Family Background and Intelligence on Tenth-Grade Boys* (Ann Arbor: University of Michigan Institute for Social Research, 1970), pp. 62-71; and Marvin E. Olsen, "Social and Political Participation of Blacks," *American Sociological Review* 35 (August 1970): 682-97.

2. On assimilation in American life and religious attendance, see Hart M. Nelsen and H. David Allen, "Ethnicity, Americanization, and Religious Attendance," *American Journal of Sociology* 79 (January 1974): 906-22.

3. Gerhard Lenski, *The Religious Factor*, rev. ed. (Garden City, N. Y.: Doubleday & Co., 1963), p. 329.

4. Rodney Stark and Charles Y. Glock, *American Piety: The Nature of Religious Commitment* (Berkeley: University of California Press, 1968), p. 19.

5. Ibid., pp. 179, 181.

6. Joseph E. Faulkner and Gordon F. De Jong, "Religiosity in 5-D: An Empirical Analysis," *Social Forces* 45 (December 1966): 252.

7. Lenski, *Religious Factor*, p. 18.

8. Richard R. Clayton, "5-D or 1?" *Journal for the Scientific Study of Religion* 10 (Spring 1971) :39.

9. For example, see Howard M. Bahr, Lois Franz Bartel, and Bruce A. Chadwick, "Orthodoxy, Activism, and the Salience of Religion," *Journal for the Scientific Study of Religion* 10 (Summer 1971): 69-75.

10. Lenski, *Religious Factor*, p. 329.

11. Ibid., pp. 73-74.

12. Charles Y. Glock and Rodney Stark, *Religion and Society in Tension* (Chicago: Rand McNally, 1965), pp. 20-21.

13. Stark and Glock, *American Piety*, p. 16.

14. J. Milton Yinger, *The Scientific Study of Religion* (New York: Macmillan, 1970), p. 27.

15. Lenski, *Religious Factor*, p. 25.

16. For his dimensions, see Lenski, *Religious Factor*, pp. 23-25. The quotation is from Hart M. Nelsen, Raytha L. Yokley, and Thomas W. Madron, "Rural-Urban Differences in Religiosity," *Rural Sociology* 36 (September 1971): 390.

17. A similar procedure was followed in an analysis of residential differences among whites; see H. Nelsen, Yokley, and Madron, "Rural-Urban Differences," pp. 390-91.

18. Glock and Stark, *Religion and Society in Tension*, pp. 39-66.

19. Hart M. Nelsen, Raytha L. Yokley, and Anne K. Nelsen, eds., *The Black Church in America* (New York: Basic Books, 1971), p. 9. See also E. T. Krueger, "Negro Religious Expression," *American Journal of Sociology* 38 (July 1932): 25, 29-30.

20. Samuel S. Hill, *Southern Churches in Crisis* (New York: Holt, Rinehart, and Winston, 1967).

21. H. Nelsen, Yokley, and A. Nelsen, *Black Church in America*, p. 9.

22. The South includes Alabama, Arkansas, Delaware, the District of Columbia, Florida, Georgia, Kentucky, Louisiana, Maryland, Mississippi, North Carolina, Oklahoma, South Carolina, Tennessee, Texas, Virginia, and West Virginia. In this study, unless otherwise indicated, "no responses" were deleted from the analysis. Individuals not responding to a given item were few in number, and the magnitude of such deletion (which is assumed to add no undue bias to the study) can be estimated by comparing the N given as part of each table with the size of the sample (the data sets utilized in this study are listed in Appendix B) when the table is not limited to Protestants only.

The two sets of factors generally employed in analysis have already been introduced. For the effects of particular variables upon religiosity, the reader may want to see Gerhard E. Lenski, "Social Correlates of Religious Interest," *American Sociological Review* 18 (October, 1953):533-44; and Bernard Lazerwitz, "Some Factors Associated with Variations in Church Attendance," *Social Forces* 29 (May 1961):301-9. In examining racial differences the following predictor variables are employed except in several instances where additional factors are added for reasons to be made clear later in the study: race, education, region, and residence.

Where appropriate, examination of racial differences is limited to Protestants. For example, the items comprising the ideological dimension indexes are especially suitable for Protestants and do not tap as well ideological differences among Catholics. At each place in the study where an analysis is reported, the respondents are identified if the analysis does not include the entire sample.

The Gallup Organization has used national probability samples since at least 1952 and the present design of the sample is that of "a replicated probability sample down to the block level in the case of urban areas and to segments of townships in the case of rural areas" (see *Gallup Opinion Index*, Report 78 [December 1971], pp. 27-28). The sampling procedure is designed to be representative of the adult civilian population residing in private households. Sampling tolerances are given by the Gallup Organization (see *Gallup Opinion Index*) and a comparison of recommended allowance for sampling error of a percentage (as given by the *Index*) with the results of the MCA test for significance for eta coefficent indicates the acceptability of using the latter means of testing for significance. For a discussion of systematic error and sampling variability associated with poll data gathered by the various polling organizations see Norval D. Glenn, "Problems of Comparability in Trend Studies with Opinion Poll Data," *Public Opinion Quarterly* 34 (Spring 1970):82-91. While the results of probability testing are shown in this study, the reader should give more attention to sizes of coefficients (eta and beta) for relationships, since the method of probability testing employed here technically depends on simple random sampling, a criterion not met by the data. An exception is the Bowling Green study reported later.

Prior to about 1960 the Gallup data sets did not include separate black, other nonwhite, and white identifications. Only white-nonwhite categories were used in the coding of the racial identities. Consequently, in the use of these early data, the nonwhite-white categories are utilized; when used together with later surveys (with the same question appearing in both earlier and later surveys), the nonwhite-white categories were employed. In employing only the more recent data, black-white identifications have been utilized, and other nonwhites are deleted in the analysis. A list of Gallup surveys employed in this study, together with sample size information, is found in Appendix B.

Finally it should be noted that the strategy employed was to determine racial differences by utilizing factors already introduced in this study. Since the Gallup surveys include about 10 percent of the total size of sample as black or nonwhite (there are only a handful of nonwhites who are nonblack in any given Gallup survey for which there is the more complete racial identification), the influence of the predictor variables (excluding race) could generally be seen separately for whites and blacks (or nonwhites) simply by rerunning the tables for blacks (or nonwhites) only. Because of the already heavy computer time use by this study, separate tables for whites were not run, except in several instances where interaction was clearly occurring. White-only tables would strongly resemble the tables for the total sample (that is, whites together with blacks or nonwhites), since 90 percent of the total sample is white.

23. For a discussion of the absence of residential differences among whites in this dimension of religiosity, see H. Nelsen, Yokley, and Madron, "Rural-Urban Differences," pp. 392-94.

24. Hill, *Southern Churches in Crisis*, p. 153.

25. Norval Glenn, "Negro Religion and Negro Status in the United States,"

in *Religion, Culture and Society*, ed. Louis Schneider (New York: John Wiley and Sons, 1964), p. 623.

26. Ibid., p. 625.

27. Krueger, "Negro Religious Expression."

28. Glenn, "Negro Religion," p. 629.

29. Ibid., pp. 631-32.

30. Ibid., p. 633.

31. The items (with the positive-answer scores) were: (A) Do you believe that Jesus Christ was the Son of God or just a man?—Son of God (89.9 percent so responding); (B) Do you believe that there is or is not a life after death?—Is (74.8 percent); (C) Do you believe that there is or is not a devil?—Is (61.8 percent; and (D) Do you think that a person can be a Christian even if he doesn't believe that every word of the New Testament is true?—Uncertain, No (33.6 percent). The method of scaling as modified by Robert N. Ford ("A Rapid Scoring Procedure for Scaling Questions," *Public Opinion Quarterly* 14 [Fall 1950]:507-32) was adopted; because one item fell outside the 80-20 maximal percentage range, item A was deleted in recomputing the coefficient of reproducibility, which was again found to be at the acceptable level of .95.

Using only the responses from the black interviewees, the coefficient of reproducibility was .96; and all the items were positively interrelated, with the mean value for phi coefficient being +.31 (one relationship was not significant at the 5 percent level—literalism and Jesus—with phi = +.08, but this was because of extreme marginals). The four items were used for the final index, and thus a range of 0 through 4 was possible.

32. The four items (with the positive responses) were: Now here are some questions on religion; which of the following do you believe in? (A) Life after death?—Yes (73.2 percent); (B) The devil?—Yes (59.2 percent); (C) Hell?—Yes (65.0 percent); and (D) Heaven?—Yes (85.2 percent). A fifth item—reincarnation (19.4 percent yes)—was excluded from the start as not being related to Christian ideology. Concerning life after death, of the respondents to the 1957 survey, 74.8 percent replied affirmatively, compared to 73.2 percent of the respondents in the 1968 survey. Giving an affirmative response to the question concerning the devil were 61.8 percent in 1957 and 59.2 percent in 1968. These percentages seem remarkably stable over time.

33. Here, rather than using the technique of Guttman-scaling, inter-item and item-total correlation coefficients were computed. The items were highly intercorrelated, with product moment correlations between +.44 and +.77, with responses of "no opinion" counting as negative replies. The items were also highly intercorrelated (+.46 through +.78) when "no opinions" were deleted. For the black respondents only, all inter-item correlations were significant at the 5 percent level and ranged between +.28 and +.73 (mean intercorrelation = +.45), using phi-coefficient. J. P. Guilford (*Fundamental Statistics in Psychology and Education*, 4th ed. [New York: McGraw-Hill Book Co., 1965], p. 481) suggests that the intercorrelations range between +.10 and +.60. All met the minimal level. Again using product moment correlation, the item-total correlations were computed, and these ranged between +.73 and +.87 (+.73 and +.88 with deletion of "no opinions"). Here Guilford suggests a range of .30 and .80; and, again, the minimal level was met. In sum, the index was judged to have internal consistency. Unless otherwise noted, responses from white Protestants and Catholics were utilized in these cross-tabulations.

34. H. Nelsen, Yokley, and A. Nelsen, "Rural-Urban Differences," p. 392.

35. Lenski ("Social Correlates," p. 535) noted that "women are generally more interested in the activities of religious groups and participate in them with greater frequency than men." In American society the woman's interests are generally more concerned with the home and raising the children; closely related is the role of religion, including church attendance and prayer. Similarly, Lazerwitz ("Some Factors," p. 308) reported that Christian women go to church more often than Christian men.

36. Lenski, *Religious Factor*, pp. 25, 39-40, 57-58.

37. H. Nelsen, Yokley, and A. Nelsen, *Black Church in America*, p. 8.

38. Ibid., p. 10.

39. Lenski, *Religious Factor*, pp. 39-41, 49.

40. Nicholas Babchuk and Ralph V. Thompson, "The Voluntary Association of Negroes," *American Sociological Review* 27 (October 1962):650.

41. It was desired to examine differences in attendance by age at this point in the study. Differences in attendance over time will be included in the discussion of the findings from a trend analysis of attendance in the last chapter.

42. When the data to be analyzed includes both white Protestants and white Catholics, as well as nonwhites, regional and residential differences disappear.

43. The items were: (A) Who was the mother of Jesus? (B) Where was Jesus born? (C) What is the first book of the Bible? (D) What country ruled Jerusalem during the time of Jesus? (E) Who delivered the Sermon on the Mount? (F) Could the respondent name one or more major prophets mentioned in the Old Testament? and (G) Could the respondent name who wrote most of the books in the New Testament? In an earlier analysis of residential differences for whites (H. Nelsen, Yokley, and Madron, "Rural-Urban Differences," p. 391), the individual items were positively interrelated, with inter-item correlations ranging between +.10 and +.40 and with coefficient alpha being .70. For a discussion of alpha see J. P. Guilford, *Psychometric Methods* 2d ed. (New York: McGraw-Hill, 1954), pp. 380-81; see also Guilford, *Fundamental Statistics*, pp. 458-62. For black respondents the inter-item correlations ranged between +.08 and +.71 (mean intercorrelation = +.33), using phi-coefficient; and all but two were significant at the 5-percent level. The two intercorrelations not reaching the level of significance had extreme marginals.

44. Gary Marx, *Protest and Prejudice*, rev. ed. (New York: Harper & Row, 1969), p. 101, footnote 17.

## Chapter 5

1. Gary T. Marx, *Protest and Prejudice*, rev. ed. (New York: Harper and Row, 1969), p. 105; see also in Hart M. Nelsen, Raytha L. Yokley, and Anne K. Nelsen, eds., *The Black Church in America* (New York: Basic Books, 1971), p. 158.

2. Donald Young, *American Minority Peoples* (New York: Harper and Brothers, 1932), p. 529.

3. Marx, *Protest and Prejudice*, p. 97; see also in H. Nelsen, Yokley, and A. Nelsen, pp. 152-53.

4. H. Nelsen, Yokley, and A. Nelsen, *Black Church in America*, p. 12.

5. E. Franklin Frazier, *The Negro Church in America* (New York: Schocken Books, 1964), p. 55.

6. Ibid., p. 85.

7. Singer has defined *ethnogenesis* as a "process whereby a people, that is an ethnic group, comes into existence." He notes that the process involves the development of separate social structures, a growing awareness of "commonality of fate," and the possible continued development of the ethnic group. See: L. Singer, "Ethnogenesis and Negro-Americans Today," *Social Research* 29 (Winter 1962):423-24.

8. For a discussion of the black middle class as "the most advanced element in the process of integration" and as essentially churchless, see Frazier, *Negro Church*, p. 85.

9. The "Puritan ethic" or "Puritan morality" includes a "strong condemnation of such worldly vices (or pleasures) as drinking, dancing, gambling . . . [and] abstention from these practices is a mild form of asceticism . . . that is practiced by many orthodox religious groups but is especially prevalent among fundamentalist sects," according to Thomas R. Ford, "Status, Residence, and Fundamentalist Religious Beliefs in the Southern Appalachians," *Social Forces* 39 (October 1960):43.

10. H. Nelsen, Yokley, and A. Nelsen, *Black Church in America*, pp. 12-13.

11. For the 1957 responses, the *voluntary* response (discussed in the previous section of this chapter) was inversely coupled with approval of the church expressing views (eta = -.11) and conservative religious ideology was positively related to approval of the church expressing views (eta = +.17), but the relationships were not significant at the .05 level, owing to small sample size (only the nonwhite responses were analyzed here).

12. We are reminded here of Jeffrey Hadden's thesis that there was a "gathering storm" in the white churches by the late 1960s, with the laity increasingly wanting ministers to stay out of politics. See Jeffrey K. Hadden, *The Gathering Storm in the Churches* (Garden City, N.Y.: Doubleday & Co., 1969).

13. It might be noted that in a reanalysis, attendance was added as a predictor variable. There were no significant differences between church attenders and nonattenders on attitude toward the march. The data were run only for blacks. Religiosity (as measured by attendance) was not operating here to dampen militancy.

*Chapter 6*

1. Kenneth B. Clark, *Dark Ghetto* (New York: Harper and Row, 1965), p. 176; also in Hart M. Nelsen, Raytha L. Yokley, and Anne K. Nelsen, eds., *The Black Church in America* (New York: Basic Books, 1971), p. 145.

2. Clark, *Dark Ghetto*, p. 182; also in H. Nelsen, Yokley, and A. Nelsen, *Black Church in America*, p. 149.

3. Gary T. Marx, *Protest and Prejudice*, rev. ed. (New York: Harper and Row, 1969), pp. xxvi-xxvii.

4. Gary T. Marx, "Religion: Opiate or Inspiration of Civil Rights Militancy among Negroes?" *American Sociological Review* 32 (February 1967):67-68.

5. Ibid., table 5, p. 69.

6. Ibid., table 6, p. 69.

7. Ibid., p. 70.

8. Ibid., pp. 71-72.

9. Ibid., p. 72.

10. Marx, *Protest and Prejudice*, pp. 94-105; see also in H. Nelsen, Yokley, and A. Nelsen, *Black Church in America*, pp. 150-60.

11. Ibid., p. 99.

12. Ibid., p. 101, footnote 18.

13. Ibid., pp. 100-101.

14. Russell R. Dynes, "Church-Sect Typology and Socio-Economic Status," *American Sociological Review* 20 (October 1955):560; N. J. Demerath III, "In a Sow's Ear: A Reply to Goode," *Journal for the Scientific Study of Religion* 6 (Spring 1967):84.

15. N. J. Demerath III, *Social Class in American Protestantism* (Chicago: Rand McNally, 1965).

16. Furthermore, it can be shown that there are substantial relationships between subjective importance assigned to religion, orthodoxy of belief, and attendance at worship services (the values for gamma coefficient are, in order, +.59, +.51, and +.40, and all are significant at the .001 level of probability); consequently, variance on sectarianism which has not been controlled through excluding members of sects and cults and which is part and parcel of the orthodoxy variable will also affect the relationships between subjective importance assigned to religion and militancy and between attendance at worship services and militancy. The above coefficients resulted from reanalysis of the Marx data.

17. In a preliminary analysis age and occupation were shown to be generally unrelated to militancy when these other variables were utilized as predictors. Concerning the wisdom of including the residential variable, see Hart M. Nelsen, Raytha L. Yokley, and Thomas W. Madron, "Rural-Urban Differences in Religiosity," *Rural Sociology* 36 (September 1971):389-96; and Hart M. Nelsen and Raytha L. Yokley, "Civil Rights Attitudes of Rural and Urban Presbyterians," *Rural Sociology* 35 (June 1970):161-74. The inclusion of income and residential background gave little more explanatory power, however.

18. For an introduction to the church-sect typology and two individual orientations of religiosity, see Hart M. Nelsen, "Sectarianism, World View, and Anomie," *Social Forces* 51 (September 1972):226-33.

19. Demerath, *Social Class*, pp. 37-38.

20. Gunnar Myrdal, *An American Dilemma* (New York: Harper & Row, 1944), p. 877.

21. The view here is of the black church vis-à-vis the black community rather than in relation to the white society. From the latter perspective, the black "church" in accommodation to (white) society would reject a protest role. Myrdal and others have recognized the potential of the black church by taking the former perspective.

22. The concept of a "proreligion" variable stems from Gordon W. Allport and J. Michael Ross, "Personal Religious Orientation and Prejudice," *Journal of Personality and Social Psychology* 5 (April 1967):432-43. Allport and Ross compare individuals who are nonchurchgoers, people with intrinsic religious orientations, those with extrinsic religious orientations, and people who are indiscriminately proreligious in terms of prejudice level.

23. "Detroiters were ranked high in devotionalism if (a) they reported praying more than once a day, plus asking what God would have them do either *often* or *sometimes*, or if (b) they reported praying once a day, but *often* asking what God would have them do." Gerhard Lenski, *The Religious Factor*, rev. ed. (Garden City, N.Y.: Doubleday, 1963), p. 58.

24. Demerath, *Social Class*, p. 64.

25. Attendance is used by Demerath as an item in the churchlike religiosity index rather than in the sectlike religiosity index, although he does note that it is the "least church like" of his items (*Social Class*, p. 78). It is to be remembered that it was attendance that was employed (in addition to devotionalism) in the reanalysis of the Lenski data; and it is precisely this variable that would bridge the gap between churchlike and sectlike orientations. The wording of the item for subjective rating of religion suggests that it is more sectlike than churchlike: "All in all, how important would you say that religion is to you—extremely important, quite important, fairly important, not too important, or not important at all?" The word "important" suggests personal piety, alternate wordings perhaps giving quite different results would include "How much interest do you have in religion?—Much, Some, Little, None" (this item is from Lenski) or "How important to you is participating in a local church?—Extremely . . . not at all." Lenski's wording might well give a more balanced assessment of the saliency of religion to the individual respondent. The third item is related to saliency of religious involvement.

26. The six items from Lenski (*Religious Factor*, p. 56) are: (1) Do you believe there is a God, or not? (2) Do you think God is like a Heavenly Father who watches over you, or do you have some other belief? (3) Do you believe that God answers people's prayers, or not? (4) Do you believe in a life after death, or not; if so, do you also believe that in the next life some people will be punished and others rewarded by God, or not? (5) Do you believe that, when they are able, God expects people to worship Him in their churches and synagogues, *every* week, or not? (6) Do you believe that Jesus was God's only Son sent into the world to save sinful men, or do you believe that he was simply a very good man and teacher, or do you have some other belief?

27. Lenski, *Religious Factor*, p. 57.

28. A word on procedure regarding "no responses" is necessary here. Lenski apparently counted lack of response to a given item as "heterodox" (or lack of orthodoxy), whereas here lack of response to one or more items meant that the respondent was considered ineligible in the assignment of hetero-doxy-orthodoxy labels unless that respondent was heterodox because of an item he or she actually answered. Counting ineligible respondents here as heterodox, 56.5 percent of the 405 black respondents were orthodox.

29. For (white) differences in religious ideology by region and by size of city, see H. Nelsen, Yokley, and Madron, "Rural-Urban Differences," as well as earlier portions of this study.

30. With the exception of one intercorrelation ("life after death" and "expect people to worship"), the values for Q coefficient for the intercorrelations ranged between +.23 and +.97 (three were spuriously 1.00 due to one cell having zero frequency in the four-cell cross-tabulation, with the exception being +.05). In sum, the orthodoxy index has internal reliability and from an inspection of the content of the items, appears to have validity.

31. Earl D. C. Brewer, "Religion and the Churches," in *The Southern*

*Appalachian Region: A Survey*, ed. Thomas R. Ford (Lexington: University of Kentucky Press, 1962), pp. 205, 207.

32. The four items (with the positive responses) are: (1) Testifying about one's religious experience should be a part of regular church services—strongly agree and agree; (2) Do you believe that God sends misfortune and illness on people as punishment for sins?—Yes, Unsure; (3) Here are four statements which have been made about the Bible [and] I'd like you to tell me which is closest to your own view: (a) The Bible is God's Word and all it says is true . . . ; and (4) Some people feel a minister should have, above all else, training for the ministry. Other people say that training is less important than his feeling a call to the ministry. How do you feel on this question?—Feel a call, unsure, have both.

In order, the percent of respondents replying positively were: 60.2, 62.8, 88.2, and 91.4, with percentages of "no responses" being, in order, 3.2, 1.2, 4.7, and 1.5. The "no response" problem was handled here in the same way it was handled for orthodoxy.

Respondents were coded as low or high on sectarianism, with only one negative response necessary for low categorization. The first two items quite clearly carried the weight of the scale. The first item concerning testifying should uncover a respondent's preference for more direct emotional involvement in the worship service; it is also indirectly associated with the concept of the "saved," for those who testify are, in effect, claiming an exclusive membership. The second question deals with the perception of God as an exacting and righteous judge, which is an Old Testament viewpoint.

33. H. Nelsen, "Sectarianism."

34. The first four of the items of this religious ideology scale (used in part here) are: (1) I think it is more important to go to church than to be active in politics: strongly agree, agree; (2) We have all been taught the Ten Commandments and we know of other scriptural statements concerning what we should do. Which of the following statements comes closest to your feeling about the Commandments? (a) The Commandments are to be followed because they are rules God has given us in order to lead Christian lives; and (b) The Commandments give us a general idea how to live, but we must interpret them ourselves to fit the situation—the first response is conservative; (3) Would you tell me whether you think drinking is always wrong, sometimes wrong, or never wrong?—always wrong; and (4) Here are four statements which have been made about the Bible. I'd like you to tell me which is closest to your own view. (a) The Bible is God's Word and all it says is true . . . . The two sectarianism items (concerning testifying and God as sending misfortune) comprised the fifth and sixth items here and were designated as tapping the sectarianism end of the scale.

For the black Bowling Green respondents the value of Q coefficient for the relationship between the two sectarianism items was +.33 (significant at the .05 level), and the values for Q for the relationships among the first four items ranged between +.38 and +.54 (all significant at the .05 level).

35. The interrelationships between the four sectarianism items ranged between +.20 and +.50, with one relationship (testifying and training) only approaching .05 significance and with the other interrelationships significant at the .05 level (one-sided).

Computation of alpha using Kuder-Richardson Formula 20 gave a value for the coefficient of .33 and the point-biserial item-totals were, in order, +.68, +.71, +.44, and +.43, and these fall within the .30 and .80 range suggested by Guilford. On alpha and the point-biserial range, see J. P. Guilford, *Fundamental Statistics in Psychology and Education*, 4th ed. (New York: McGraw-Hill, 1965), pp. 458-60, 481.

36. Demerath, *Social Class*, p. 77.

37. Two points were given for belonging to two or more organizations. One point (each) was given for belonging to one outside organization, attending regularly, and reporting an officership. The resulting scores were collapsed as follows: (0 points) score 0; (1 point) scores 1-2; and (2 points) scores 3-4. This part of the index ranged, then, from 0 through 2.

38. One point (each) was assigned for replying positively to the first item and for replying two or three times a month or more. This part of the index ranged from 0 through 2. The scores from the two parts were added, giving one point each for scores 1-2 for each subtotal. The index thus ranged from 0 through 2.

39. The three items were: (1) I enjoy working in church activities—agree, unsure, disagree; (2) Church activities such as meetings and committee work are a major source of satisfaction in my life—agree, unsure, disagree; (3) I keep pretty well informed about the church I attend and I have some influence on its decisions—agree, unsure, disagree. One point (each) was given for agreeing to each item, with a resulting range of 0 through 3.

40. The values for the gamma coefficients for the interrelationships among the items for the churchlike involvement measure ranged between +.27 and +.99 and were all significant at the .05 level. Similarly, the values for the Q coefficients for the additional measure's items ranged between +.72 and +.95, and all were significant at the .05 level.

41. One point was assigned for one, two, or three friends, and two points were assigned for four or five friends.

42. In order, one point (each) was assigned for the responses "much," "more," and "agree." The scores for this part of the index were collapsed as follows: (0 points) scores 0-1, (1 point) score 2, and (2 points) score 3. Thus on both parts the scores ranged from 0 through 2 and these were added together to give an index ranging from 0 through 4.

43. Demerath, *Social Class*, p. 77.

44. For this second measure three items were utilized: (1) Having adult Sunday School classes talking about social and political issues—should not do this, unsure, should do this; (2) Letting nonchurch groups use the building for meetings to discuss community issues—should not do this, unsure, should do this; and (3) Working to convert men to Jesus Christ and not getting involved in political matters—should not do this, unsure, should do this. In order, one point (each) was assigned for the responses "should not do this," "should not do this," and "should do this." The second measure thus had a range from 0 through 3.

45. Values for gamma for the interrelationships among the sectlike involvement items ranged between +.30 and +.71, and all were significant at the .05 level. Similarly, values for Q for the interrelationships among the religious over political items ranged between +.21 and +.70, and two of three of these were significant at the .05 level (the third, which approached significance, involved the first and third items).

165

46. The eight items, including the positive response and the percent so responding, based on the total N of 405 ("no responses" are included as negative replies), are:

Greater political power for Negroes—*strongly approve, approve,* undecided, disapprove, strongly disapprove (82.9 percent)

Would you say that the Civil Rights Demonstrations over the last few years have helped or hurt the Negro's cause?—*helped,* made little difference, hurt (70.4 percent)

Negroes are pushing too hard for equal rights—strongly agree, agree, undecided, *disagree, strongly disagree* (62.7 percent)

In your opinion, is the government in Washington pushing integration too slow, too fast, or about right?—*too slow,* too fast, about right (52.6 percent)

Black Power means that militant Negroes are trying to stir up rebellion—strongly agree, agree, undecided, *disagree, strongly disagree* (40.5 percent)

Black Power is a legitimate response to white power—*strongly agree, agree,* undecided, disagree, strongly disagree (35.5 percent)

The Black Power Movement, in general—*strongly approve, approve,* undecided, disapprove, strongly disapprove (28.2 percent)

The Civil Rights Movement, in general—*strongly approve,* approve, undecided, disapprove, strongly disapprove (16.3 percent)

47. Using standard scoring for Guttman scaling, the coefficient of reproducibility with "no responses" removed was .90; with "no responses" counted as negative the coefficient was .89. The value of alpha (using Kuder-Richardson formula 20) was .69, with missing data deleted, and .70 with missing data counted as negative. With deletion of missing data, the item-totals had point biserial coefficients ranging from +.36 through +.66; with missing data counted as negative replies the item-totals had coefficients ranging from +.41 through +.65. With missing data removed, all intercorrelations between items were significant at the 5 percent level (two-sided), and the values for Q coefficient ranged from +.36 through +.75, with the mean value being +.52.

48. Of the 382 respondents who could be classified on militancy, 40.6 percent were placed in the high category, or scoring positively on five or more items.

49. The results of the analyses summarized in these and subsequent tables are not appreciably changed with the introduction of the additional controls utilized earlier in the study.

50. When respondents with missing data on the orthodoxy and sectarianism indexes and respondents not identified with a local religious body were deleted from the analysis, the results were substantially the same as those reported in this section.

## Chapter 7

1. L. Paul Metzger, "American Sociology and Black Assimilation: Conflicting Perspectives," *American Journal of Sociology* 76 (January 1971):628.

2. For an introductory discussion of this process, see L. Singer, "Ethnogenesis and Negro-Americans Today," *Social Research* 29 (Winter 1962): 419-32.

3. Raymond Breton, "Institutional Completeness of Ethnic Communities

and the Personal Relations of Immigrants," *American Journal of Sociology* 70 (September 1964):193-205.

4. Gayraud S. Wilmore, Jr., "The Case for a New Black Church Style," *Church in Metropolis* 18 (Fall 1968):19, also in H. Nelsen, Yokley, and A. Nelsen, *Black Church in America*, p. 326.

5. Clifton F. Brown, "Black Religion–1968," in *In Black America, 1968: The Year of Awakening*, ed. Patricia W. Romero (Washington, D. C.: United Pub. Corp. for the Association for the Study of Negro Life and History, 1969), pp. 348-49; also in H. Nelsen, Yokley, and A. Nelsen, *Black Church in America*, p. 22.

6. Charles V. Hamilton, *The Black Preacher in America* (New York: William Morrow & Co., 1972), pp. 172-76, 180-81.

7. Wilmore, "Case," p. 20; also in H. Nelsen, Yokley, and A. Nelsen, *Black Church in America*, p. 328.

8. James H. Cone, *Black Theology and Black Power* (New York: Seabury Press, 1969), pp. 112, 108-9; also in H. Nelsen, Yokley, and A. Nelsen, *Black Church in America*, pp. 351, 348-49.

9. Cone, *Black Theology*, pp. 112, 114; also in H. Nelsen, Yokley, and A. Nelsen, *Black Church in America*, pp. 351, 353.

10. Robert Lane, *Political Life: Why People Get Involved in Politics* (New York: Free Press of Glencoe, 1959), pp. 245, 251.

11. Ibid., p. 25.

12. Figure 1 was first discussed in Anne Kusener Nelsen and Hart M. Nelsen, "Keeping the Faith in the Sixties: The Black Christian Response to the Revolution and Beyond" (Paper read at the eighty-sixth annual meeting of the American Historical Association, New York, December 28, 1971).

13. Marvin E. Olsen, "Social and Political Participation of Blacks," *American Sociological Review* 35 (August 1970):692.

14. The larger data set was employed for two other secondary analyses; for a more extended discussion of the data set see: Hart M. Nelsen, "Intellectualism and Religious Attendance of Metropolitan Residents," *Journal for the Scientific Study of Religion* 12 (September 1973):285-96; Hart M. Nelsen and H. David Allen, "Ethnicity, Americanization, and Religious Attendance," *American Journal of Sociology* 79 (January 1974):906-22.

15. Jack Elinson, Paul W. Haberman, and Cyrille Gell, *Ethnic and Educational Data on Adults in New York City* (New York: School of Public Health and Administrative Medicine, Columbia University, 1967), p. 221.

16. Jack Elinson, Elena Padilla, and Marvin E. Perkins, *Public Image of Mental Health Services* (New York: Mental Health Materials Center, 1967), pp. 154-95.

17. H. Nelsen, Yokley, and A. Nelsen, *Black Church in America*, pp. 8-9. Italics added.

18. In other locales, especially metropolitan cities of the North, orthodoxy may act in a more conservative manner and in those settings a different measure (one linked with churchlike involvement) may be desired.

19. Carleton L. Lee, "Religious Roots of the Negro Protest," in *Assuring Freedom to the Free*, ed. Arnold M. Rose (Detroit: Wayne State University Press, 1964), p. 70.

20. Benjamin E. Mays and Joseph W. Nicholson, *The Negro's Church*, (New York: Institute of Social and Religious Research, 1933), p. 70.

21. Ibid., p. 72. Italics added.

22. Ibid., p. 92.
23. Ibid., p. 93.
24. J. Milton Yinger, *The Scientific Study of Religion* (New York: Macmillan, 1970), p. 342.
25. Gary T. Marx, *Protest and Prejudice*, rev. ed. (New York: Harper & Row, 1969), p. 104; also in H. Nelsen, Yokley, and A. Nelsen, *Black Church in America*, p. 157.
26. William Brink and Louis Harris, *The Negro Revolution in America* (New York: Simon and Schuster, 1963), pp. 100-101.
27. Milton M. Gordon, *Assimilation in American Life* (New York: Oxford University Press, 1964), p. 76.
28. Alphonso Pinkney, *Black Americans* (Englewood Cliffs, N.J. Prentice-Hall, 1969), pp. 179-81.
29. This statement takes a lot for granted. On this point Carmichael and Hamilton write:

Some believe that there is a conflict between the so-called American Creed and American practices. The Creed is supposed to contain considerations of equality and liberty, at least certainly equal opportunity, and justice. The fact is, of course, that these are simply words which *were not even originally intended* to have applicability to black people: Article I of the Constitution affirms that the black man is three-fifths of a person. The fact is that [white] people live their daily lives making practical day-to-day decisions about their jobs, homes, children. And in a profit-oriented, materialistic society, there is little time to reflect on creeds, especially if it could mean more job competition, "lower property values," and the "daughter marrying a Negro." There is no "American dilemma," no moral hang-up, and black people should not base decisions on the assumption that a dilemma exists.

See Stokely Carmichael and Charles V. Hamilton, *Black Power: The Politics of Liberation in America* (New York: Alfred A. Knopf and Random House, Vintage Books, 1967), p. 77.

For an earlier, lucid analysis of the Myrdal hypothesis—that there is conflict between selfish interest and commitment to the American Creed—see: Ernest Q. Campbell, "Moral Discomfort and Racial Segregation—An Examination of the Myrdal Hypothesis," *Social Forces* 39 (March 1961): 228-34. Campbell observes that "certain virtues valued especially in middle and upper class white culture operate to check the pace of social change that the flow of guilt would initiate were these other things not valued."
30. Benjamin E. Mays, "The Negro Church in American Life," *Christendom* 5 (Summer 1940):397.

*Appendix A*

1. R. L. Polk Co., *Caron's Bowling Green City Directory* (Detroit: Caron Directory Publishing Co., 1969).
2. Charles H. Backstrom and Gerald Hursh, *Survey Research* (Evanston, Ill.: Northwestern University Press, 1963), pp. 50-58.
3. U.S. Bureau of the Census, *Census of Population: 1970, General Population Characteristics*, Final Report PC(1)-B19 Kentucky.
4. A further description can be found in *Caron's Bowling Green City Directory*; see Julia Neal, "Bowling Green," pp. xi-xviii.

# INDEX

African Methodist Episcopal Church (A.M.E.): founding of, 19-20
Allen, Richard, 20
Andrews, Frank, 156 n.1
Argyle, Michael, 2
Assimilation: civic, 136; cultural and structural, 14; and depoliticization, 6; and desire for civil rights-oriented religion, 14
Assimilationist perspective: of black church, 8-9, 100-102; of racial change, 2; and study of black religion, 136. *See also* Black church: models of

Babchuk, Nicholas, 10, 75, 149 n.39
Baptist religion as sectarian, 3
Black church: as accommodating needs of black masses, 3; as agency of uplift, 39-40; as anti-intellectual, 5; and apprehension of whites, 19; assimilationist perspective of, 8-9, 100-102; as authoritarian, 55; Baptist, 25-26; as barrier to integration, 5; as causing isolation of blacks, 9-10; in Chicago, 9, 46-50; and church name changes, 8; and class system, 27-28, 46-48, 54; and class system in rural community, 41; and communal life, 20; as community center and black institution, 10, 24, 48, 53, 83-84, 124; and community cohesion, 84; compensatory model of, 9-10; conservative-progressive split, 26;

as controlled by blacks, 1; as democratic, 11; and economics, 31-32; and education, 29-30; after Emancipation, 24; and escape from frustrations, 5; ethnic community perspective of, 11-13, 125; evolution of, 24-27; and family life, 29; finances of, 44-45; as fundamentalist, 2-3; inclusiveness of, 28; independence and defiance of, 23; beginning of independent, 19-20; and intellectuals, 54-56; leadership of, 33-34; in Lincoln, Nebraska, 10; loyalty to, 16; malleability of, 11; and militancy, 24, 54, 82-125; three models for viewing, 8-13, 125-29; and mutual aid, 25, 30-31; in New York City, 21-32; as opportunity for prestige, 9; and otherworldliness, 54; and overchurching, 45; in Philadelphia, 31; in plantation areas, 39; and pluralism, 2; as prophet to white society, 13, 126-27; as prophetic, 11; and protest, 11, 98-99; as race institution, 48; and range of services in rural areas, 41-42; resentment toward, 48-49; revitalization of, 11; role in community, 55; rural, 37-38, 41-43, 153 n.11; and self-esteem, 19, 51, 53; as semi-involuntary, 83-86; separatism and independence of, 19; and separatist stance, 46; and social control, 86-92; solidarity toward, 54-55;

Black church (continued):
soul of, 11; storefront, 5, 50-51, 154-55 n.44; strength of, 15; types of, 47; in urban areas, 43-45; written off as not concerned with social problems, 3. See also Protest
Black community as pathological, 10
Black culture. See Black community
Black Jews, 50
Black ministers: as community leaders, 29; in days of slavery, 21; as leaders of other organizations, 42; and politics, 24, 32-33, 49; as prophetic to white society, 11; as protest leaders, 5; as race men, 57, 125; in rural area, 38-40; status in rural community, 43; views of conservative, 34
Black Muslims, 51-52
Black Panthers, 8
Black power movements: lack of studies on, 2
Black religion: Africanisms in, 17, 22-23; and dream of abolition, 21; interpreted as sectarian, 3; of lower-class urbanites, 70; and passive submission of slaves, 21; and protest, 134; stereotype of, 58, 67-69. See also Protest; Slave religion
Blacks: and participation in social and political activities, 12; as sectarian, 2; in voluntary associations, 10; in white churches, 126
Bowling Green, Kentucky, 110; sample, 141-43
Breton, Raymond, 6
Brewer, Earl D. C., 110-11
Brink, William, 135-36
Brotz, Howard M., 51
Brown, Clifton F., 126
Butler, Jon, 24, 28, 32

Catholic Church: in Chicago, 47
Cayton, Horace R., 9, 46, 47-49, 154-55 n.44
Church: definition, 3 n; and immigrant, 6; and political interests of members, 129; membership as nominal in rural areas, 41
Church attendance, 74-78, 128-32; and assimilation, 16; interpretation of, 78-79; traditional view of, 61. See also Religiosity, dimensions of
Church of the Black Madonna, 8
Church-sect, 106; forms of involvement of, 112-15; and social change, 3
Clark, Kenneth B., 100-101, 125
Clayton, Richard R., 64
Cleage, Albert, Jr., 8
Coleman, James S., 8
Communalism: black churches as developing, 7
Community cohesion among blacks, 8. See also Black church: as community center and black institution
Cone, James H., 126-27
Cultural shock theory, 4

Daniel, Vattel Elbert, 46-48, 55
Data employed in the study, 144-46, 157-58 n.22
De Jong, Gordon F., 64
Demerath, N. J. III, 103, 105, 107-9, 112, 114
Denmark Vesey plot, 19, 23
Devotionalism, 64. See also Religiosity
Drake, St. Clair, 10, 46-49, 154-55 n.44
Du Bois, W. E. B., 20, 28-29
Dynes, Russell R., 3 n, 4

Educational level and sectarianism, 7
Ethnic community: development of, 7-8
Ethnic status. See Minority status

Faulkner, Joseph E., 64
Fauset, Arthur Huff, 3, 50-51
Felton, Ralph A., 153 n.11
Frazier, E. Franklin, 5, 8-9, 22-24, 27, 29-30, 55-56, 83, 100, 102, 124-25

Racial comparisons (*continued*):
sion of religiosity, 69-72; intellectual dimension, 79-80; religiosity, 63, 80; ritualistic dimension, 72-78; religious phenomena, 1
Ransom, Reverdy, 33-34
Religion: as encouraging political interest, 6; influence in American life, 133-34; saliency of, 64-65
Religiosity: basis of, 61-62; church attendance, 128-32; churchlike and sectlike, defined, 3 n; definition of, 1 n; dimensions of, 63-65; dimensions used in this study, 65; experiential dimension of, 66-69; expressive and instrumental forms of, 108; ideological dimension of, 69-72, 110-12; intellectual dimension of, 79-80; local church variation of, 103; measures of orthodoxy and sectarianism, 106-12; and militancy, 101-5; multidimensionality of, 64; proreligiosity, 107; ritualistic dimension of, 72-78. *See also* Church attendance; Devotionalism; Militancy; Orthodoxy; Prayer
Religious beliefs: and intrinsic cultural traits, 14; of migrants to the city, 4-5; unidimensionality of, 4
Religious ideology: and migration to city, 4-5; and rural background, 4-5; and social class, 4
Religious phenomena: comparison of black and white, 1
Richardson, Harry V., 14-15, 39-40
Rossi, Peter, 2
Rural background of church members, 4
Rural church: membership and Holiness preference in city, 49-50. *See also* Black church: rural
Rural communities and religiosity, 62

Sample, 141-43
Sectarianism: and aggression, 135; definition of, 7 n; measure of,

110-12. *See also* Religiosity; Religious ideology
Sect-church typology. *See* Church-sect
Sex roles and religion, 61
Silberman, Charles E., 9
Slave religion, 17-24; Africanisms in, 21-24; and black minister, 20-21; and communal life, 20; and control by whites, 17-18; and creation of separate black church, 19; as imparting sense of dignity, 19; on plantation, 18; in urban North, 19
Social issues. *See* Racial comparisons: on church addressing social and political issues
Social problems addressed by black church, 82-83
Sonquist, John, 156 n.1
Spear, Allan, 46, 49-50
Spirituals and protest, 5
Stark, Rodney, 63
Stereotype of blacks as sectarian, 92
Storefront church. *See* Black church

Thompson, Ralph, 10, 75, 149 n.39
Turner, Nat, 18, 23

Variables employed in this study, 59-61
Vesey, Denmark, 18-19
Voluntary association membership, 149 n.39. *See also* Blacks

Wade, Richard C., 18-19
Washington, Booker T., 29, 33
Washington, Joseph R., Jr., 13
Whitt, Hugh P., 5
Wilmore, Gayraud S., Jr., 13, 126-27
Woodson, Carter G., 24, 30, 32
Wright, Charles R., 149 n.39
Wright, R. R., Jr., 34

Yinger, J. Milton, 135
Yokley, Raytha L., 3
Young, Donald, 1, 5
Youth: alienation of, in rural black church, 38-39